SONS AND MOTHERS

WHY MEN BEHAVE AS THEY DO

PAUL OLSEN

M. Evans and Company, Inc.
New York

Library of Congress Cataloging in Publication Data

Olsen, Paul.
 Sons and mothers.

 1. Mothers and sons. 2. Men—Psychology. 3. Love,
Maternal. I. Title.
HQ759.062   155.9′24   81-1844

ISBN 0-87131-338-3   AACR2

M. Evans and Company, Inc.
216 East 49 Street
New York, New York 10017

Design by Diane Gedymin

Manufactured in the United States of America

9 8 7 6 5 4 3 2 1

SONS AND MOTHERS

For Deborah

And to the memory of Phil Ochs:
My son, my son, my sailor from the sea . . .

CONTENTS

ACKNOWLEDGMENTS

My particular thanks to Fred Graver, whose editorial talents are no less than spectacular. His care with, and respect for, this book have formed one of the most gratifying experiences of my writing life. And my deepest gratitude to my friend Herb Katz, without whose presence there would have been no book at all.

My daughter, Marissa, and my son, Matthew, must know that without their existence I would have a little less hope for the generations to come. And I would want my mother to know that so much of what follows in these pages was born from the infinite complexity of our relationship.

Also, my deepest gratitude to those people, women and men, who come to my office and share their sadnesses and joys with me. Their anonymity has, as usual, been scrupulously preserved—and I have focused not upon their histories but upon their stories.

Finally, my thanks to three men who have given me their unflagging devotion and support: Peter Prudden, Jonathan Weiss, and Paul Zola.

ONE

"MEET MY MOTHER"

The way in which men see the world, the people in it—all the relationships they are ever likely to have—is welded to the bond with their mothers. This bond, this relationship, is the cornerstone of all future relationships. Yet it is a bond infused with and surrounded by misunderstandings, fears, and a dark, almost unfathomable mythology. It is perhaps the most misunderstood, misconstrued, and puzzling relationship of all, because by the very process of being reared in its mystique men can barely see it at all; there seems almost to be a prohibition against seeing it clearly. And its confusions are compounded by a pattern of thoughts, behaviors, and actions—a collusion between mother and son dictating that neither be allowed to see the other for what he or she is, and that neither be allowed to see into the core of the relationship and its staggering implications.

For ages we have been trying to see and explain this relationship with sense and "logic"—but with a logic conditioned and shaped by that relationship itself. And so of course we have not been able to see it clearly. We have been getting only hints, and most of these hints have emerged from situations and contexts that have somehow gone "wrong," where the mother–son bond has been damaged, where it has led to emotional disturbances and major problems in living.

Perhaps to see this relationship more clearly is to lead to the deflation of its myth, and perhaps in the past we have needed too strongly to keep that myth alive and thriving. And keeping the bond shrouded in myth, none of us—women nor men—can ever get at its possibilities, its real human possibilities.

In our society the man is forced, impelled, to grow up, to leave mother behind as if she were some transient and finite aspect of childhood. Which is an impossibility. There is no high steel fence separating man from child. No one can take such a quantum leap from one stage of life to another; but it may give many of us comfort to think so, to think men have grown up fully, have shucked their dependency.

Yet everything is still there in the chronologically grown man—everything felt, experienced, and learned from day one, including the need for mother, for Woman. In the East the idea of wholeness assumes that the totality of these experiences is alive within the man; he must simply rediscover their aliveness to achieve wholeness and to realize his place in the universe. Here, in the West, we fragment our lives into seemingly neat (but unreal) conceptual packages and pigeonholes. We define ourselves as people by what we do, by our status symbols, by our beliefs—but rarely by what we *know* or by what we *are*.

If this model were not inadequate, if it were not corroded at the core, why are there midlife crises of despair and frustration and feelings of personal emptiness and absence of meaning? Why do men and women search so desperately for someone of the opposite sex to *make* them happy? Why is there such heavy traffic in alcohol, marijuana, tranquilizers, momentary bliss as a substitute for real happiness and connection?

Yet there *is* a search here, a search for wholeness in what appears at first glance merely to be an escape from the stress and pain of "adult" life. We want to get the fragments back together, to regain a sense of unity, peace, of personal meaning and purpose.

Clearly, a man's life in our culture is based upon the shifting sands of roles and postures, but this fragmentation is deliberately cloaked by an illusion of solidity emphasized by social and economic productivity. It is all a bit like taking a walk on slippery stones poking through the surface of a stream—maintaining a precarious balance while only vaguely sensing the potential meaning of a tumble into the flow of the stream. Men tend to stay on the surface, to step from one fragment, one role, to the next: almost nothing flows, living is like a halting movie film played one static frame at a time. Men are one way at work, another way at home, another way with male friends, still another way with women.

There is chaos in this fragmentation, a confusion, a despair, a profound anxiety. A man wonders who he is, what he is doing. He must, as the British were once fond of saying, "carry on"—but with what, to what end, for what purpose?

I am going to emphasize that a man's most important task is to reconnect the fragments of his life, to attempt to gather back to himself the split-off aspects of his existence. And to attempt this task requires a reappraisal of his relationship with his mother—the beginning of his life, a relationship in which wholeness exists for at least some period of time before it begins to break off into pieces.

To rethink and reformulate the mother–son relationship—to deprive it of its mythology—is to run the risk of restructuring completely the way we see the world, the way we relate to what we have always believed to be reality, the way we touch others. Before any such risk is taken, a man must realize that the way in which he sees the world is the way in which his mother saw and sees it—a world constructed for him by her vision of it, *her* reality. He was born into it. There was no choice.

We are going to take that risk here—a risk that every man must take. Almost like a poet, he must take the existing *mythos*, the way things seem, the way things are accepted wholesale, and rearrange all of it until he can craft his own life—making his life his own, welding the fragments.

Let us enter the relationship of mother and son, discovering its pains and its almost infinite possibilities.

From that bond of incredibly awe-inspiring closeness and oneness, the long contact of flesh on flesh, feeling upon feeling, through which is poured all the hopes and dreams, anxieties and failures, of the mother, from the communication of feeling through the flesh itself, there begins to develop in the child a vision of existence, of the world, that he will come to believe is true, real, the only world there is. He begins even to "know" who his father is through the world-view of his mother—"knowing" this long, very long,

before he has the intellectual equipment and critical judgment to bring his own perceptions to appraise with any
clarity at all the identity and worth of his male parent.
And even when he finally has developed some critical
faculties he will be appraising his father through the world-
view, the value system, of his mother, the architect of his
world. Initially, then, his critical judgment is not even
fully his own.

As the Jungian psychiatrist and mythologist John Weir
Perry suggests, even the old-fashioned classic Freudian
Oedipus complex, that apparently eternal "triangle," is
probably at heart a two-party interaction: mother and son,
with the third leg of the triangle being the *image* of the
father as communicated nonverbally, then verbally, by the
mother to her son.

What is communicated to this child is a *whole world*
perceived and interpreted by his mother: the whens and
wheres of pleasure and pain, the identity of the father, the
good guys and the bad guys, the blacks and whites and
sometimes the grays, the fears and securities. All these
arbitrated by a mother, like a deity, the great goddess, for
good or ill. A world of possibilities or impotence, optimism
or pessimism, a world grown over with lush gardens or a
world fragmented by darkness and threat—more often by
both. A world of sanity, madness, or just plain being alive
in it to take one's chances and see what comes.

This is power. Ultimate power. And myths are always
woven from power, spun from it with countless variations
and textures, with threads of love, hate, yearning, disenchantment, and often a baffling perplexity of design. And
a lifelong struggle for freedom from this world is begun;
a struggle to keep the good and exorcise the bad, to discover a new world while searching for the answers to the

riddles of the first relationship men have ever had, the only world men have ever known.

As the boy grows, as other worlds intrude, he finds fault with his first world, particularly if he does not like what he has become and has the honesty to face the fact that he does not like it. Or he stays entrenched in the myths, swallowed by them, because exposing them would leave him altogether without a world and without the strength to create another. Or he attempts to build new myths structured on the old fantasies. A man often thinks that he can become a man in his own world; but except in rare, even remarkable, cases he must to his mother be no more (and no less) than *her* son in *her* world.

From a mother's perspective the balance required here can be nothing short of miraculous, an incredible tightwire act. She must all at once try to let her son go and clutch him to her—to help him become a man and to keep him a boy.

Her shaping of him will be directed by attitudes both conscious and hidden—attitudes toward men in general, husband and father in particular; by her sense of the world as largely a good or a hostile place; by the way she sees herself in relation to this larger world. These attitudes are breathed into life by the powerful emotions that accompany and permeate them, and when communicated to her son are done so both nonverbally and verbally.

A mother will witness the process and direction of her shaping across roughly four overlapping stages, one gradually shading into the next, each new stage retaining elements of the old:

1. The earliest stage, where her fantasies and attitudes, joys, fears, and hates, will be communicated primarily nonverbally, though accompanied by words. The child

coos, grins, or frowns back, is handled, washed, and fed. The fantasies are still mainly in his mother's head—but she begins to communicate them through the way she looks, moves, holds, touches (attitudes of acceptance or rejection of male genitals often emerge here), by the way she talks, her tone of voice rather than the meaning of her words.

2. The boy's developing ability and desire to explore, think, understand language, link certain behaviors to praise or punishment. His playmates are largely chosen for him by his mother; boys and girls are judged "good" or "not good" for him. This is a period of tremendous activity on the mother's part. She is now monitoring the larger social world with its diversity of people, roles, mores, and norms. She approves of some, condemns others.

3. The boy's entrance into the more mature world of dating, sexuality, career plans, attempts to discover his "own" identity. He is learning from his own experiences more than ever before, and much of this experience may stand in contradiction to his mother's view of the world.

4. The man, living in the larger world. The struggle of self-development, the necessity to leave aspects of his mother's world that can no longer help or support him, that because of their childish nature can only hinder him.

And the mother must cope with it all, often perplexed, suffering the loss of *her child* each step of the way, suffering the pain (and sometimes feeling the joys) of her own necessity to change. At best she senses that by letting her son go she will still have him in a real and meaningful way, that she will be included in *his* world. At worst she clings to him and debilitates him through her fear of losing him— and she will *of course* lose him either through flight or through an alienating rage.

Often she cannot let go, cannot admit that her son has created a world of his own, a happiness not of *her* making. She may perceive his functioning well in the larger world, the world outside her bond with him, and this perception leads her to feel that she is on the verge of losing him forever. She desperately struggles to regain control, to pluck her son from his world and wedge him back into her own.

This, he thinks, is going to be a lovely day. An afternoon party for a few carefully selected friends, some psychotherapist colleagues and old acquaintances, a singer who enjoys performing at parties. And the guests of honor are his parents, who magically are going to be incorporated into his world. And why not? It seems a good world, much of his making and made pretty well: relatively successful, socially acceptable, large new apartment, even a bright, pretty little daughter to show off. He is, of course, making a show for his parents.

Meet my mother, he is going to say. *Meet my mother.*

And it seems to go well. Everybody talks, seems to have a good time. Good music, good food, good drink. Ice tinkles in glasses, plenty of chuckles. They all stay late and he gets a good sense of having shown his mother part of the quality of his life, his profession, his friends, his house.

The next day his mother telephones. Not to tell him that she had a good time at his party but to tell him that he is obviously unhappy. She says it is obvious because he drank too much. He listens and is hurt. Of course he is hurt. He has struck out. He has tried and failed, his fantasy of introducing his mother into his world of no more substance now than the dust motes that skitter across a sunbeam sluicing through a partly open blind.

Meet my mother . . .

Ah, for a man to make his mother his lady. His guest of honor. To squire her. To take her to lunch or dinner in a smashing restaurant. To introduce her to his friends. To, in fact, date her—to impress her as he has tried or will try to impress some other woman in his life. Somehow, by the power of a Merlin, to try to cancel out or realign or recast all those years of his dependency, his infantile bonding to her. To become a man with her and not some primitive Freudian oedipal devil who clubs his father to death in order to sleep with her.

Simply to be a man with her. To be seen as a man.

Is there a man who hasn't burned with this wish—in whom it still doesn't burn or flicker? The wish, the dream, may be reshaped or altered or punctured by psychotherapy, self-awareness, some flash of explosive insight. But is it ever snuffed out? Is the flame ever entirely dead? Does he ever really want to see that candle with its cold, lonely, charred wick? And does this disappointment always have to be?

Perhaps, just perhaps, there might be other possibilities.

A man might try to understand what his mother experiences—that as he cannot give up his world entirely to reenter hers, so too he cannot expect her to relinquish her world. He might realize that their worlds cannot, by definition, be *radically* different *at root*, that there are commonalities that beg for exploration. That somewhere, in some form, there is a point of convergence, a meeting place, a territory of mutual accommodation.

A man might try to understand that his mother has come to depend on *him* even while she must continue to relate to him as a son who can never truly stop needing the kind of love and relatedness that she feels only a mother can offer. And this is clearly one of the lingering diseases of our entire culture: when a woman becomes a mother she is not, despite all the lip service to the contrary, really supposed to be anything else. This has traditionally been the source of her power in a culture that gives her no other means of finding her place in the world. Until she is truly liberated, what else can this type of mother do when her primary role, her very identification with it, indeed her very identity, is threatened with termination? She feels it as a murder.

And a man might realize that if he is still so reliant upon the approval of his mother, then he is also still as dependent as a little boy and so is doomed to relate to his mother from this position.

Other possibilities? If a man accuses and excoriates his mother for all his disappointments and feelings of damage, then he must also accept that she is responsible for all that he likes about himself.

My mother may simply wish to remain my mother no matter what direction I take. And I will have to accept that or fight illusion all through my life. And lose the fight.

Yet what cripples the possibilities, what leaves a man caught up in a pattern of repetitive hurt, is precisely this tendency to blame, to accuse. Not to see what *is*—but only to rail against what isn't. "Why can't she accept me as a man?"

But it isn't her responsibility to give permission to be a man. A man can't ask her for permission or blame her because she withholds it—because then he is simply giving her power. And then he is back in the mother/little boy bond, crying that oft-heard lament on analysts' couches: "Why can't she *let* me be a man? Why won't she accept me?"

To blame is to avoid, to miss the point of exactly what is happening in the relationship—to miss what is happening precisely when it is happening. Blame avoids the confrontation—and so nothing is seen, nothing new is felt, nothing understood. Because blame perpetuates the struggle and abets the one-sided balance of power. Blame is a refusal to grow up, to *take* manhood, to permit a woman her motherhood. The man then misses the meaning of the event itself, the meaning of the encounter. "It shouldn't have happened!" Yet it did. But *what* happened? All the man can see are the same repetitive old responses and frustrations—but he misses the meaning of it all. If he can see the meaning, then he can understand that he is not simply a frustrated little boy.

He will be her little boy again as he was when he was five years old and she bought him a sack of marbles and urged him for the first time to go out and play with the neighborhood boys.

He came back to her in tears, the little sack empty, all his marbles lost in a game he didn't know how to play. He never knew people won or took things from you. She never told him. He came back and she comforted him. Get it off your chest. She said that a lot. Get it off your chest.

At that moment he never wanted to go out again. Never again.

But a mother doesn't grasp the core of her son's fantasy, his romantic yearning, his desire to keep her at the center of his heart. She has absolutely no idea or sense that by his yearning, his later desire to squire her and mount a show for her, he is telling her that he is really still so much in *her* world, that he wishes to enter it willingly, that by making her the focus of his wish, the object of his desire, she is as important now as she was when he clutched that little empty sack in his fist.

And yet it is so clear: mother is *still* the center, the most important human being in her son's life—and a man can march through an entire lifetime behaving and thinking that it isn't so. He can grow up, build a career, marry and have children, arrange for his mother's funeral, die. And through it all she will always be the most crucial, most dynamic, and most powerfully influential force in his life. It will happen if she is a good mother, a bad mother, an indifferent mother, a sane mother, a crazy mother. That is where she is going to stay: in the center. That is where she was in the beginning and that is where she will remain—elevated upon the pedestal of a virgin deity or hated and plunged into the depths of hell. Lucifer was a fallen angel—and they are two sides of the same coin. Good or evil, the power is still there.

It can be no other way. The bond, once formed, is never broken. But its power does not have to be binding; it needn't imply a master–slave relationship. The power *is*, and because it exists it can be seen for what it is. Perhaps with minimal value judgment. It just *is*.

A bright, attractive, witty, and very successful woman executive, who is also the mother of a nine-month-old son, is at a business lunch with a male colleague. Although business is being done, there is a casual air to the lunch—some forays made into feelings and

personal lives. Talk turns to mothers, to children, and
as she talks of that other aspect of her life, her life
as a mother, some sort of almost horrified recognition
dawns on her. She pauses, says: "I just caught myself
making plans for my son. Future plans." She muses
for a moment. "Good God, he's only nine months
old!"

The revelation almost ends business for the day:
some shaking insight has struck this unusual woman
with great power. She has suddenly seen the enormous influence she holds over her infant son, already
molding him to fit some ideal image she has of men,
of what men should be.

"He's only nine months old!" She is struck with
this fact, with the sudden knowledge that this molding, this shaping, this creation of her son's inner
life and identity has begun so early. And she is awe-
struck by this power, by the anxiety and responsibility
inherent in how she will use it.

Several days pass. She phones her lunch partner
and says, "It really hit me, that talk we had. It's
literally frightening. I'm filling my son with my own
fantasies and ideals and I think I'm already *responding* to them, to what *I'm* making of *him*. And he's
responding to what he thinks is the real me. But *is* it?
Is this what I really want?"

This is part of the power of the first relationship—and
these are the lines along which it is drawn. The beginning
phase of becoming the mother's man.

TWO

"YOU CAN'T DIVORCE YOUR MOTHER"

The first world of the boy, the world of his mother, is not an abstract world. Only the theories of it are abstract. It is a concrete world, a world of particular qualities, infinitely subtle and gross by turns. Each mother's world is like a crystal of myriad facets—the mass of the crystal being the root in the commonalities of human existence, the facets her own individual desires, wants, conditioning, dreams. Her world is populated with its own brand of good and evil, heroes and villains, has its own special structure of morality and value judgments.

The one requirement, the one fact, in the world of all mothers, whether feminists or Victorian prudes, is that the child be a child, *is* a child, in her world. And into that child, into that *son*, will be filtered, by an alchemy we still know little about, all the ingredients of the world his mother has lived in privately and publicly: all that she has experienced and gotten second-hand, all that she knows and believes without knowing, all that she remembers and has "forgotten," and all—as the Jungians and Eastern philosophers would have it—that belongs to the larger fabric of human existence. The light, darkness, myths, lies, truths, and even passions of which she may not have the faintest awareness in her conscious life.

It is a world she has come to define as real—the *only* reality. To her, as to everyone, there is no other world that is real or acceptable; she believes that her world is *the* world.

And into that world of the mother the child will arouse unaccustomed feelings, stimulate new perceptions, simply because he now exists. And whatever newness he introduces into her world will be molded to fit the system that already exists. So that from the moment he enters his mother's arms he will be accounted for, explained, and interpreted by the existing rights, wrongs, and structures of the world she has always known and believes to be a pure and true reflection of the large world that *is*. However active or passive his own budding personality, he is nevertheless plastic. He will be shaped and molded into what *ought* to be, what *should* be; rarely, if ever, will he be treated as what he is. (On a blatantly obvious level, we all remember the damaging practice of insisting that left-handed children learn to use their right hands.)

The mother will be attacked by inner angers and resentments never before felt; strange sexual feelings will be aroused by mouth on nipple. If these have been acceptable possibilities in her world, she will let herself experience them without anxiety or guilt, but if these emotions have not existed in her world she will bury them—only to fester inside her. Obviously the broader and deeper the mother's individual world, the more sensitive, the more accepting she will be of the new experiences and feelings, and the more accepting she will be of her son and of herself. She will accept her experiences as human ones—*fully* human ones. The narrower and shallower her world, the more chaos and confusion will result—and the greater the efforts to wrench the child into conformity with that world.

This is early stuff, the relation between mother and child in the first days of infancy, when most future patterns will be shaped, when a particular way of being and living begins to be imprinted. Whatever crops up in this early relationship will be dealt with by the rules of the mother's world—and, as I have said, it is done without words. Without the use of language, without conscious volition, her world begins to be communicated, taught to the child, woven into every fiber of the child's life. And as we will see, the differences between boys and girls in this setting are striking, remarkable.

In a therapy session a woman says, "I'm very upset. I feel like some kind of freak. I don't know if I can nurse Billy anymore."

"How come?"

"I'm thinking of switching him to a bottle."

"Why?"

"I don't really know how to say it. It makes me feel bad just to think of it. It's just not normal. It isn't normal, is it?"

"I don't know what to say unless you tell me."

She cries a bit, wrings her handkerchief—painfully puzzled, almost frightened. "Nursing him is . . .

well, it's some kind of sexual experience. I never had
that with my daughter."

"What did you feel with her?"

"Oh, close, warm—you know."

"Billy literally turns you on?"

"No, I can't really say that . . ."

"Maybe it's the same feeling. Maybe you just look
at boys and girls very differently. Compartments in
your mind, definitions. With a girl it's close, with a
boy it's sexy."

It had never occurred to her.

What *had* occurred to her was the notion that similar,
even identical feelings were "sexual" in relation to a boy
child but "close, warm" with a girl child. From the moment she made this *apparent* distinction—a distinction
that resided purely in the world of her thoughts, as she
had been *conditioned* to think—there was little doubt that
she would regard, train, and shape her two children in
entirely different directions: the boy would become sexual
and aggressive and therefore on some level threatening, the
girl would be "safe" and passive.

This is basic, crucial stuff. The thoughts and ideas and
fantasies that color a mother's world, especially in relation
to the sex of her children, will determine two issues at
least. One, how she will regard them and train them when
control is totally in her hands and, two, how she will *react*
to them when they provoke some feeling in her for which
she has not been prepared.

A great deal has been written about these early phases
of mothering—good writing, bad, indifferent, some valiant
but uselessly speculative, some highly imaginative and even

poetic. But what we are most concerned with here is the way in which the boy child is shaped: how that is done, what form it takes, where the roots of the process are embedded. How he gets to be the man he becomes because of the components of his mother's world. Ultimately he develops into the man he is largely because he becomes the living embodiment of that which his mother wishes and fantasizes men to be—or not to be. Everything from a hero to a villain—or a heroic villain or villainous hero. From strength to weakness. And very often she tries to make him into the man she wished she married and didn't —or into the man she once thought she married but didn't. The images she forces him to conform to frequently emerge from disappointment in her marital partner.

A question arises quite naturally at this point: What happens when a woman, bringing up her son, has a good relationship with both her husband and her father? Chances are—and I will address this more fully later on— that she will allow the male figures in her life to partake more actively in the bringing-up process. Actually, if the relationships are good, the men will want to share in the process without being asked or badgered.

The mother's positive experience with the men in her life will be more consistent with her inner images of men— and consequently she will be less compelled to "invent" a boy-man, to force him into the mold of a fantasied inner image. And it will be easier for the boy: he will sense acceptability and consistency.

But each person merely occupies a point on a continuum: no one is all good or all bad. No external perception of a man, however positive, will perfectly match the idealized inner image. I have come to believe (and I have learned this from women) that no matter how positive a woman's relationship with a husband, lover, or father, the inner image of the man will differ from external reality to a greater or lesser extent. This disparity does not always have toxic effects. Also, being human, we are dreadfully imperfect, yet our desire for perfection has an odd persistent power. We can, we think, always make a new relationship "better."

And we must not forget that in relating to a boy child, a woman is not dealing with a grown man, an adult with adult power. It bears repeating that when the boy is born it is the mother who has power—largely the power of possession.

Because her boy child is *hers*. He belongs to her. She possesses him. Forever. Even if her marriage should end in divorce, he is hers to keep; even the law tells her so. She has ultimate authority over a life. Unlike her husband, who was once a stranger, and may come to be a stranger once more, this boy was born of her, is made up of her essence. He can never be a stranger even if someday he is alienated from her; she can invoke the tie of blood.

She has *conceived* him. And in the very fabric of that word is contained the germs of imagination and fantasy. Some of the roots of the word itself revolve around concepts of "imagination," "opinion," "thought"—and "conceive" can also mean to "take into the mind." It is clear that when something is conceived, whether an idea, a project, a novel, a child, imagining and fantasy come into play and *must* come into play.

Her child is conceived and is created, it is a human life and an idea, a concrete, breathing reality, a work of the imagination, and a fantasy. All at the same time.

So the concrete, breathing boy child is born, and immediately laden with all the fantasies and notions that permeate his mother's sense of what a man *is* and *ought to be*. All her conceptions of what a man is, isn't, and must be. And here we have the beginning of it all.

The best and worst seldom happen. The mother–son relationship is usually a subtle interaction, between letting go and grasping—and that is what makes the process and the understanding of it so infinitely complex.

They are having a quarrel, the young man in his middle thirties and his mother. He is in the morass of a complicated and angry divorce, and something about the way he has been describing it, his feelings of helplessness, of being attacked, of being extracted from, has caused his mother to launch an assault on his wife. And he resents it because it makes him feel like a fool. She is telling him that she has always known that the woman he married was "beneath him," a manipulator—and that he would not heed his own mother's advice to reject her before they married.

She becomes relentless and he explodes with anger, tells her that, as with his wife, it might be best if they don't see each other for a while. He can't bear the fighting; he needs some kind of comfort and all he gets is criticism. It might be best if they put some distance between them.

Summoning a strange, almost deadly calm, she replies, "You think you can do that, do you? You think you can deal with me the same way you dealt with your wife? You can just move away, not see me, not talk to me, as if I were just another person in your life? Well, let me tell you something, my dear: you can divorce anyone you please but you'll never be able to divorce your mother. It isn't possible. We're the same flesh, the same blood. You can think a divorce is possible, but it's not. Only a fool could ever think he can divorce his mother. *It just isn't possible.* Even if you tried with every ounce of strength you have—it just isn't possible."

The same flesh, the same blood—and saying that, she strikes the chords of a truth beyond refutation, and the chords are so loud, so deep, that no reply will make any sense whatever. She is right: a man can *think* that a divorce from his mother is possible, but when he lives it out, tries to act on it, he finds it is impossible, that the memories and thoughts will cease only momentarily, that the connection will be there, hour after hour, day after day, beating and pulsing within his body as if they were after all connected with the same blood, the same flesh, not metaphorically but in hard reality—a symbiosis, an odd kind of twinship, a Siamese joining of organs and membranes, thoughts and perceptions.

A man must attempt to grow out of the infantile aspects of this relationship, but he cannot divorce his mother, though she seems often to have the power to divorce him.

A man, but a very special man, a man who seems to have risen above his mundane humanness, transcending it to a position of godliness: only such a man can strip his queen-mother of some of her attributes—but the divorce of *mother and son* can never be effected. A mythic Egyptian Horus, betrayed by his mother, Isis, who works against the independent judgment and accomplishment of her son, is able to seize the crown from her head and deny her rank—but that event took place in a world of gods and goddesses, and a man would have to become a god in order to see so clearly and stand free of the bond that keeps him imprisoned in an infantile state.

There can be years of separation, years of silence, and the bond will not be weakened by one thread. It is the fantasy, the dream and the wishing within man, that thinks he can pry free; but something inside him also says that this total freedom is not possible—that no real divorce, whether by design or by the inevitability of death, will ever make a profound break in a bond established in such a powerful, dynamic way. Men may try to deny the bond, to pretend that it has no power, attempt to diminish its importance—and be condemned to live out a lie. Because denial is flight and running away avoids the self-confrontation necessary for growth and awareness.

When a man attempts to flee his mother, he closes down; he attempts to substitute emotional awareness with physical distance—an absurd confusion of functions. He runs in terror and rage instead of pausing to understand that freedom from his dependency is a task of the inner life precisely because he is dealing with emotional and psychological factors, not with physical imprisonment—although he may *feel* that physical nearness to his mother is toxic. He must also realize that his emotional liberation requires a balance of the "good" as well as the "bad." In other words, a man must come to realize that the positive aspects of his self-identity have been achieved not only *despite* his mother's influence but also largely *because* of it. As one of my colleagues expresses it: "A mother often provides the very material of rebellion and insight while she appears to be hanging on. Someday she may appreciate it, or she may never know about it at all."

Speaking of her relationship with her son, a mother says, "I'm sixty-seven now. That's a lot of life, but I'm glad I got here because for the first time in all these years the storm is over. We seem to know each other now, and I'm not exactly sure how it happened.

"Oh, I can recollect moments, sharp, painful moments. Like the way I told him to go to hell, that he was nothing I'd ever wanted him to be, and that it was obvious that *I* wasn't what he wanted *me* to be. And I said that I could live with it, and if he couldn't it was just too bad. 'Do what you want,' I told him, 'but just stop blaming me. Just do what you want to.' "

She is a sculptress now, a very good one, a talent that bloomed after the death of her husband. She points to an unfinished piece of stone and says, "Like that. It's raw stuff and you must make something of it, not attack it. Your life is something you need to forge, to create, to find. You can't do it by smashing away at it or running from it.

"Well, he must have done something about it. He doesn't have to thwart me anymore. He's lost his need to hurt me and blame me, and I've lost my need to make demands on him. And that's the core of it."

James Joyce, one among many writers, struck the theme resonantly in *Ulysses*, where the young artist Stephen Dedalus is incessantly reminded by his friends that he refused to kneel and pray at the bedside of his dying mother. But this, too, is symbolic: the new young god divesting his mother of her queenship. And it is a wish; there is no evidence that Joyce ever did such a thing in the reality of his nonartistic life, in the other reality of mundane earthly existence.

There is, indeed, little evidence that any man has ever done such a thing, or would—unless he had lost some sort of basic humanity, unless he were crazed with rage or found that his survival depended upon such a refusal, his survival in that case being the crucial necessity to remain sane.

The woman was right; a man cannot divorce his mother.

There are certain "reasonable" explanations why this can't be done—but they are explanations put forth in the framework of a "logic" that is grotesquely far removed from the actual event, the actual meaning. For example, men are too guilty to effect the divorce, afraid of some sort of retaliation; or, on the "mature" side of the coin, too responsible, too unwilling, as good people, to deny the needs of their mothers. And all this will have an intellectual, rational cast to it—yet, on closer scrutiny, we see that they are merely following what they have been taught to believe, trained to believe, as they have been conditioned by verbal means, by the eternal verities and values communicated to us in a daily series of lectures and sermons.

And very little of it will hit the mark.

A man's life in the world is tied to that other life in the world in way that we are not even on the border of understanding without the crutch of one dense theory after another, one negating another, one trying to supplement another. We cannot get directly at the quality of that bond; we can only infer from it. We cannot enter the experience of a child; we infer from the child's behavior, and these inferences have traditionally been made by psychotherapists who guess at what is "wrong," what has gone wrong, in a situation the "rightness" of which still remains one of the great occult mysteries.

We "know" what has gone wrong. We haven't the

faintest idea what is "right." And that, for example, is why we think that pleasure is the absence of pain. Pain is what we know about—and therefore pleasure can only be its opposite.

These are thoughts. The reality of it all is mostly nonverbal.

The bond is communicated—cemented and embellished —by the contact of body on body, skin on skin. And where this breaks down, so too does the bond—not only the bond, but the humanness, the ability to live. The presence or absence of possibilities in the life of a man will to a large extent be based on the quality of contact he has had with his mother's flesh, with the satisfaction or frustration derived from her flesh, from the degree of security and warmth and possibilities that her flesh offers him. Without its positive, life-giving contact he becomes a living skeleton, soulless, pessimistic, depressed, frightened; with too much of it he becomes helpless, a perpetual child. But no one knows what is *enough*, what is the good and proper amount.

It is a fact, not a theory, that without maternal contact of any kind, orphaned children may develop a condition of depression and apathy known as *marasmus*, and can wither and die from it as a result. And we know that monkeys deprived of contact with their mothers will cling to terrycloth mother substitutes and have subsequent failures of socialization and sexual functioning. And we can view films that show withdrawn schizophrenic mothers feeding their children while holding them like broken dolls and pushing them away—investing the experience with so much anxiety and/or indifference that the future destruction of their children carries a guarantee.

So we at least know that there is "good" contact or "bad" contact between mother and son—or adequate or inadequate contact, or sometimes no contact at all. And that some degree of pleasure and intimacy *must* exist in the contact—but that it is a pleasure and intimacy that may arouse fears in the mother, fears of feeling, negative thoughts arising from the values and mores upon which her own world has been built.

The warm, pleasurable contact is necessary, wholesome, life-giving—and perhaps the major factor in a mother who to a greater or lesser extent withdraws this contact is a judgmental questioning of her motivations. She becomes consumed by critical negative judgments aimed at herself. She "feels funny," anxious, confused, oddly frightened.

The wholesomeness, the *pleasure,* of the relationship is damaged or otherwise subverted precisely at the moment that the mother is first aware of being threatened by the encounter with her child. And quite likely the threat is seen as more potent when the child is a boy.

It seems that way. And it certainly seems that this kind of close contact parallels the sort of contact a grown man both needs and is frightened of, must often get away from through his cursory sexual contacts—and is yet magnetically attracted to. We will see how this plays out in sexual activity.

And there is another possibility that may stem powerfully from the closeness of the contact, the merging of son into mother, and we get it partly from Eastern religions and philosophies. This is the concept of *samadhi,* called by some *nirvana,* but always meaning the ability to leave the mundane earth and retreat inside oneself to a state, a feeling, of bliss. And where is the prototype of this bliss?

At a meeting of psychotherapists, a very prominent Eastern guru is talking about detachment, about blanking out the thinking process. He maintains that in order to "see clearly" we must give up the images we carry within us, in essence free ourselves from inner content and return to a basic, perhaps "blissful" state in which all becomes one.

The statement bothers, troubles, many of the psychotherapists present because they are related strongly to a materialistic world, strongly related to theories that stress outer, worldly reality as the only reality. And one says, "What he wants is the tit. He wants all of us to regress to the tit, like infants nursing."

The psychotherapist doesn't see all of the picture, doesn't see that his theoretical bias against "regression" is merely a value judgment and not a truth, but he is on the right track. The blissful state so desired by proponents of Eastern disciplines (and so badly confused with "enlightenment" by their Western followers) is *precisely* the ability to regress, to return *at will* and for brief moments of time, to a primal state of bliss perhaps initially experienced at the mother's breast, but more likely within the womb itself. I stress *at will* because, unlike the sudden regression to earlier stages of life that can terrify and break apart a person in the throes of psychosis or a "bad" LSD trip, this state of bliss or *samadhi* or whatever other term applies is achieved with attention and control, and can also be emerged from at will.

But there can be no such experience in adult life unless the original experience of bliss, of complete gratification, actually occurred. And that is why—because the first year of life is so crucial, the gratification so crucial—only intact people can apparently have this *willed*, drug-free, psychosis-free experience of bliss in later life. That is, they have something truly nourishing and truly "good" to regress to. Damaged people experience great terror in this attempt and are apt to fragment from it: there is nothing "good" to return to.

But you don't have to be damaged to fear this "return" or regression, even if it can be controlled.

All you must be is a man—and that is enough to stand your hair on end at the mere possibility of being asked to retreat to a state so closely approximating the flesh-on-flesh contact with mother. It is creepy, frightening, anxiety-provoking just in the thinking of it—and the first impulse is to run from any idea of it.

What a man is frightened of, more than anything else in the vast possibilities of living experience, is dependency, regression to a state in which he becomes an infant in the care of his mother—a mother later unconsciously symbolized by almost all women with whom he comes in contact.

A man may be able to *do* it, but the very thought of it terrifies him *because he knows it is possible*, because on some profound level he has never left the world of his mother. Because his unconscious *is* the unconscious of his mother and he has made frantic efforts to leave it, to become independent, to shake her.

A man spends most of his life running away from his mother's world through the pursuit of his masculine toys: he plays sports, jocks around in locker rooms, buys cars, spends his time learning how to wheel and deal financially, becomes sexually aggressive—all those driven activities which may turn a man into a parody. He can become intellectualized, using the "clean," "analytic," "logical" forms of thought and behavior to identify himself with "maleness," abandoning the intuition, sensitivity, and feeling that he defines as "female." And to cement his necessary avoidance of anything that may bring him closer to a way of being defined as feminine, society has provided him with a fear of homosexuality. To be tender is to be queer, to touch another man is to be queer, to kiss another man is to be queer—to be, that is, quintessentially feminine.

That is how far he wishes to travel from his mother. But he does it at the cost of incredible damage and waste: he buries at least half his life, lays to rest at least half his potentiality as a full human being—and will live the rest of his life in conflict, like a self divided, like a socially acceptable schizophrenic. His so-called maleness always at war with his unconscious, with what is hidden from him, with what he does not know about the deeper regions of himself—but which always gets expressed in one way or another.

Or if he is a psychotherapist he lassoes his unconscious like some wild animal, interprets it (rightly or wrongly is of no importance), and thereby gains an illusory control over it: a kind of rape of the psyche.

But the running away does no good: like Heracles he will finally fall into the oblivion of the mother sucking him back into his unawareness. It was Jung who said that mother is a symbol of the unconscious—and Jung may have been quite correct. And this is what happens to a man when he avoids a confrontation with the mother inside him, the mother absorbed into him by that original swallowing and blending of flesh.

This is what happens so often when a man retires after years of "masculine" work: he sinks back into a dependency, into the pull of the mother inside him, and he becomes like a child "looking for something to do," looking without finding because he has never once in the course of running from his inner life paused to discover what riches are within—because the within is what he cannot see, cannot "think" about or "reason" about, and so must fear. Marriage can die right here, because he is surrounded only by women—the woman inside, the darkness, the woman outside, his wife, who tries to mobilize him but who is suddenly seen as a dictator.

He has worked all his life to avoid the look within—and his work has served the same purpose as a drug. It is interesting that work has been found to have therapeutic effect on alcoholics; indeed it becomes a substitute for alcohol, and both are used to a great extent to avoid coming to terms with the life within, with the unconscious, with mother. Also interesting is that alcoholics respond more favorably to therapists who speak to them in gentle, soft tones: the words seem less important than the sound of a soothing "maternal" voice.

Work, like alcohol, is frequently the escape for a person who is already wallowing in the infantile relationship with his mother—wallowing so deeply, so painfully, that escape becomes vital or he will be swallowed. But he becomes swallowed anyway, surfeited with alcohol or surfeited with work.

Women do not seem to have this problem with the same degree of severity; they can slide much more easily into the unconscious, at least to levels where they are not so desperately threatened by the mother within. With men, the levels of threat are far closer to the surface: almost any drift into sensitivity or feeling stirs up the threat. Unless, of course, sensitivity and intuition are "tools" in their work, as among male psychotherapists or artists, whose sensitivity becomes less a part of their state of

existence than a means of earning their living. But simply
to sit, to be alone, without doing a blessed thing but being
with themselves—men just cannot do it without experiencing a profound anxiety.

Feeling is the province of the infant; then it becomes
the province of the woman. And the vast majority of men
want nothing to do with it if they can help it.

What I am underlining is that when men attempt to
escape from the world of the mother, which is the world
of what men are not aware of within themselves, their
unconscious, they take on the attributes of social super-
ficiality and so continually fall into the stereotype of the
male—the sexist male, if you wish. This is the world of
earning money, of status, of the pursuit of materialistic
symbols, of the perpetual erection—all substitutes for connecting with their inner lives.

The woman was right: a man cannot divorce his mother.
He can only discover who she is, how she is separate from
him—and come to appreciate what she has given him.

But he cannot run away from her forever. Because like
Heracles, like the protagonist of John O'Hara's *Appoint-
ment in Samarra,* he will run exactly to the place where he
will become overwhelmed, where he will die in his own
darkness.

In a moment when his guard is dropped a man can
experience something new:

"I never made love before," he says. "I just screwed.
But when it happened, it was like nothing I'd ever
experienced before. I think I must have blacked out
for a second, and all I was aware of was some kind
of incredible warmth, my whole body was filled with
it, and I didn't want to leave her or roll away from

her. I wanted to get closer to her, very close. I could feel the warmth of her body against mine, soft and gentle, and for the first time in my life I stayed in a woman's arms and fell asleep."

What he does with that experience only time will tell. He can deny it in the morning. Or he can enter it fully and never again feel the need to run away.

THREE

THE GOOD MOTHER AND THE BAD MOTHER

A boy does not grow up "clean" or, as Ernest Hemingway might have put it, "true and well." He is not nurtured and loved and cared for by an unambivalent human being who is free of all needs, warps, and selfishness. The selfless, intuitive, always warm and good mother has been a cherished myth, now gradually being laid to rest by a society suffering spasms of confusion and a knowledge that almost everything seems to be turning out badly—although you might still invite a punch in the mouth if you insult another man's mother. But in the context of what we are beginning to learn about relationships, you might get punched because your insult strikes a chord of recognition: that what you say might well be true. But mother must be good: if she isn't, then what really *is* left in the world? I will punch you for frightening me with my abandonment.

Putting to rest the myth of the all-good mother, what does it mean for a boy, a man, to be cut off from his mother? To have the image shattered, the bond frayed, to recognize for the first time and with intense force that the woman who held him, nurtured him, loved him, can also be cold, removed, critical, demanding—that she can reach almost demonic depths?

It is partly the boy's perception of his mother's demandingness and power over him that stimulates impulses to separate himself from her. If she were the legendary all-good, all-loving mother, why would he *ever* want to leave the protective womb? He must see the need, the necessity, for pulling away from her—and this drive to separation and independence occurs precisely *because* the mother, being human, is ambivalent. In varying degrees of intensity she wishes to hold on to her son, yet knows she must help him grow into manhood. But it is the holding on against which he rebels in order to seek his freedom and individuality.

I am saying that the mother's ambivalence is crucial for a boy's need to become independent. But ambivalence is a confused, unclear state of being in which almost all feelings and actions—positive and negative—appear to be expressed almost simultaneously ("I have mixed feelings about that"). Confronted with this ambivalence, the boy tries to separate the "good" from the "bad." How does he try to effect this separation, and toward what does it lead?

The recognition that begins this process of separation and independence involves a painful, at times unbearable prying away from the mother's power and domination. That process is not a simple matter of "growing up," of breaking away to embark on one's own life course, but is a far more complex process requiring the confronting of a welter of ambivalent feelings—an experience so powerful that it will color a man's relationships with all the women with whom he will ever be involved—lovers, wives, friends, business associates. And the ambivalence will shift, sometimes with dizzying speed, from pole to pole, from positive feeling to negative, and will erupt in such comments of despair as "What does she want from me?" or "Why can't I ever please her?"

The overall sense is of being cut off, rejected, on some level perhaps even unloved and slashed away from some old and needed security. Without the comfort of pleasing her comes the despair of being abandoned by her, cast out of the nest, a child in a world of adults with whom he suddenly finds it difficult to cope. And this despair, for lack of a better word, we have come to call depression.

Here we have the brutal split experienced at one time or another by all of us. This woman becomes divided: the good mother and the bad mother—the bad mother who withholds, deprives, attacks, a woman who can never be pleased. For some men, the ambivalence can become so tortuous that purely for relief and as a protection against almost going mad, they invest one woman with all the properties of goodness, another woman with all the components of evil. My wife is a demon, my lover is perfect; and when my lover shades into evil (why didn't I *see* it before?) there will be a new lover, even more perfect than the one before, to take her place. But it is only through confronting the ambivalence itself that this sort of repetitive splitting can be prevented.

Over a drink in a bar, a man says something about his wife which he might well say about his mother if he were in touch with the real architect of his life. He stares at the glass in his hand as if he hopes it will become a mystic's crystal ball.

"I can't see any way out except divorce. I've done everything she's ever wanted: bought a house that I can't afford, had three kids that I don't really want, whipped myself crazy making almost seventy-five thousand dollars a year—and yesterday she told me to sew a button on my shirt. And last week she refused to wait on a gas line and I had to get up at five in the morning to do it myself.

"Look, I don't want a woman to be some kind of housewife-slave—I don't think I ever really wanted that, but I work almost sixty hours a week at a job I don't like very much, and she wouldn't even sew a fucking button on my shirt."

He sets his glass back on the bar and uncontrollably begins to cry.

"What does she want from me?"

This is the way in which the "bad" mother is experienced by most men in our culture: driving, insatiable, uncooperative, demanding—a bitch, a demonic witch riding high on her broomstick. The wife has become the mother in her most evil aspects. And it may all repeat, in relationship after relationship. And no one saw it coming. No one could do anything about it.

No peace has ever been made with the "bad" mother, indeed most of the time there is no awareness of her at all, and what started as a marriage made in heaven deteriorates into a living hell, triggering reenactments of mother-son frustrations until all that remains is the bad mother of nightmares and fairy tales—and the urgent need to escape. But, again, escape leads nowhere.

Admittedly, we have come to a *slightly* more balanced position over the decades, after years of bitter, angry reaction against the false face of the sweet, all-suffering, all-good Mom—a reaction that has accused her of every possible psychological crime. Some time ago it was even popular to hypothesize a "schizophrenogenic" mother—a mother who gave her children psychosis as if passed through her genes like eye color and skin texture. But as with all intense reactions, it was apparently a necessary one to get closer to the truth. Even Mary Worth of the comics has been converted from a dowdy, plump, brow-furrowed, gray-haired mother to a chic older woman with new hairdo and slimmer figure. And the tentative moves toward a more balanced view have begun to suggest that men have been raised by women who are nothing more or less than human, with all the goodness, failures, problems, miseries, and distortions of the human condition itself.

But still, men continue to maintain the split because they can't stand ambivalence. Perhaps everything once seemed good, then turned sour. Perhaps the ambivalence is itself experienced as the badness; ambivalence is always a painful, tortured experience, a profound frustration.

The facade has been partially torn away, and all the demands in the relationship have been laid bare. Remove the mystique of superhuman goodness and you discover the complexity of the person. And you might not like it—just as a child sometimes devours the icing of a cake, but when he tastes the cake itself, he pushes it away. The icing is good, but the cake is too complicated in taste and texture. Why, he cries, can't it *all* be sweet?

There are enormous demands in the mother–son relationship, and neither partner is selfless: the child overtly demands his nurturance by screaming and thrashing about, and the mother, quite simply and frankly, wants a reward, a payoff. *Her* demand will be that the boy grow into the man she wants; he must grow into someone who fits her image of the ideal man. An ideal son, ideal husband, ideal lover. These are the reciprocal demands: the boy wants an ideal mother, the mother wants an ideal son. And with or without awareness—mostly without—the shaping and conditioning begin, the agenda is set. The mother may approve of some behavior as her son grows—a behavior that usually centers on loyalty, fidelity, to her; but more important, she tries to remove or punish any behavior or attitude that does not fit the ideal image of *her* man.

Grow up. But grow up to be the man *I* want you to be. This requires a difficult juggling act on her part, but one which is often oddly "successful": she strives *at the same time* to keep the child a son, a boy, and an ideal man. And this inevitably leads to those familiar frustrations experienced later in life: the maternal intrusions and criticisms of the son who is not fulfilling the demand that he be a docile, respectful, dependent, attentive son while simultaneously being a man who can make it in the world, be a source of pride to his mother, and reflect glory upon her.

And when he is seen by his mother as failing this expectation, the man shrinks back into the boy and he cannot handle the situation; and the mother, the wife, becomes "bad." All bad. He will swear she is trying to destroy him.

The man in the bar who plaintively asks, "What does she want from me?" breaks into tears and alarms the bartender and a few fellow drinkers, and indeed the mucus that trickles from his nose does give him the momentary appearance of being a little boy. He can't seem to handle the relationship with his wife. Has he ever asked, "What do I want, what have I wanted, from *her?*" It can't be as simple as rage at sewing on a button or waiting on a gas line. What *he* wants, an examination of that, would take him back to childhood, to the bad and perhaps even crazy mother—but at the moment he is aware only that he is a man in a man–woman relationship in which the woman is *the* endless source of frustration and conflict.

When he wipes his eyes and blows his nose and orders another drink, he hits the mark in a way, but in a "rational" way, still pinning his misery to his wife:

> I just want to be happy. I want a woman who can
> make me happy. I get home feeling good and she's
> down—and in ten minutes I'm down. She brings me
> down. When she's up it's terrific. She gets me up, and
> it's then that I think our marriage is worth saving.
> I like being married then. Everything can go okay for
> a while, then she gets down, her moods change like
> the wind, and without knowing how it happened I'm
> down again and I want to get out of it. Goddamn!
> I just want to find a woman who can make me happy.

The crucial point here is that, like a little boy, he wants his wife–mother to *make* him happy: he depends upon her moods, her behavior, to dictate his happiness and contentment, becomes depressed and frustrated when she is "down." And to some extent most men are like this—profoundly dependent upon some outer source for their happiness and well-being. Of course there are people, men and women, who seem impossible to live with, and in such cases divorce might be the only reasonable resolution. But it is the *power* in the wish that someone *make* us happy that keeps us so dependent, so enraged. Men want too much from women, women want too much from men, and a little is not enough.

As he sips another drink and becomes weepy again, the man in the bar has no awareness at all of his tremendous dependency on his wife. Nor does he ask what he really wants in a woman ("happiness" is a vague term; we seem compelled to try to be happy in our society); he can only brood about what he is not getting from his wife. He has no all-giving mother. And he flails about in frustration and may even get a divorce, but unless he can be made to see his childishness and understand that he is seeing his wife through the hidden screen of what he wants from a mother, he will again involve himself with a woman who will become yet another bad mother even though she may seem vastly different to him on the surface.

The demands are there: son on mother and later on wife; mother on son and later on man. A juggling act in which the juggler's hands are greased and the balls are differently sized and weighted.

It plays out directly between mother and boy:

He is eleven and he has five dollars to buy his mother a birthday present. He doesn't know what to buy, so he shops, looking in store windows, searching drug-store counters. And loses all sense of time.

Finally he buys a planter, a ceramic peacock large enough for a small snakeplant, and on the way home realizes that he is terribly late for supper.

His mother launches into a relentless tongue-lashing. About to cry, he thrusts the present at her, mumbles "Happy birthday," and tries to explain why he lost track of time. She becomes softer but says,

"You still shouldn't have been late."

She thanks him for the gift; and she deprives him of television for three days.

For years afterward he cannot look at the peacock planter without wishing to smash it to bits.

And later in life, in almost identical emotional terms, it can play out between mother and man:

She is sitting with her divorced son, who visits frequently with his children and the woman with whom he has been living for several years. They seem to have good times together, good visits, and he is obviously happier than he has ever been.

Then one day his mother says, "It would make your father and me very happy if you'd get married. You seem to love Maria, so why *not* get married? She even loves the children. It makes us sad that you're not married."

He is about to reply when she quickly adds, "But I suppose that when you get married and have a home of your own, you won't come to visit us anymore."

He experiences a pressure in his throat and a slight burning in his nose. He says, "What am I supposed to do with *that?* No matter what I do, you're saying I'll make you unhappy."

"Well, I suppose in this day and age mothers don't matter very much." Then: "Sometimes we wonder why you ever got divorced in the first place."

The frustration and rage he feels are almost overwhelming. He leaves the room, goes upstairs, and smashes his fists into a pillow in the bedroom, aware that he is crying. And the next night he dreams that he is being held fast by a many-armed woman much larger than himself, whose face he cannot see.

This mother is in no way a vicious or sadistic person, a crazy person, a willfully destructive human being. She is playing out her own problems with happiness, frustration, independence: she is afraid of what she does not know or understand—her son's life. But for her son she has played out the aspect of the bad, the terrible, mother. For him she indeed has many arms (oddly like the devouring aspect of the Hindu goddess Kali), each arm like a vise from which he cannot escape any more than he can escape her unending criticisms. No sooner does one arm seduce him into a false sense of security and pleasure, a sense that the relationship is smooth and good, than suddenly other arms seem to wind silently and unseen around his neck. She is, as his dream says, much larger than he.

When he calms down, when the anger abates, he can recognize her as basically a good person who has given much to him. And yet he is always caught off balance, surprised, by her "attacks."

So there exists in every mother a good and a terrible aspect, each playing itself out as it must. And her son will respond—as *he* must. The terrible mother also urges her son to perform great feats for her, never really letting on what it is that will finally satisfy her. ("What does she want from me?") A crucial aspect of the bad mother is that she will never inform her son what it is that she wants from him; he must try to discover this, and if he searches for the answer the search itself robs him of his independence and freedom and keeps him tied to her.

She will never tell him, and he will never find out.

The real mother, the flesh-and-blood mother, the one

who speaks on the phone, writes letters, and carries about her business in the everyday world of mundane reality, cannot tell her son what it is that she wants of him *because she does not know* that what she wants is for him to be a child again. And her son usually has only an inkling that this may be the case—but he insists on bringing to her altar the gifts of adulthood. But that is not what the "bad" mother wants. She wants her child.

A novelist friend has become not only rather successful at his craft, but has developed a fine reputation as a teacher. His four published novels have been criticized almost unmercifully by his mother.

She can be Victorian: "You ruined that book because of the filthy language."

Political: "That whole chapter sounded as if you were a communist."

Psychological: "There was a lot of whining in that book."

Ethnic: "Aren't you ashamed of saying those things about your own background?"

She never runs dry of criticism—and as he gets better and more of the world at large recognizes his talents, she becomes more pointed.

Part of why he has been driven to produce for her—and this has been a theme in his life—is finally to present her with something she will accept and admire. But she will not or cannot.

He sees her as a woman who will devour him if he does not make every effort to get away from her. He knows it will be a lifelong battle and he will cope with it by writing—by writing for himself.

As in psychotherapy, self-awareness, whatever, the clean shaft of humor does much to lighten the dark night of the soul played out in these relationships. And there are many jokes, many stories, that have an incredibly broad cultural appeal—and for some reason most of these stories are called "Jewish mother" jokes. What may have begun as a plaint by Jewish men born from some sharp awareness of their mothers has now a universal appeal: today Gentiles have "Jewish" mothers, too. Here she is in all her spiderlike glory:

> A mother gives her son two neckties for his birthday. To please her, he wears one of them when he next visits her. Noticing it, she says, "What's the matter? Don't you like the other one?"

This is the humor of heartbreak, of frustration, of anger. What does she want?

Again, I stress that whatever happens at the moment happens at the moment: in situations like this the terrible mother is playing herself out, is expressing herself because the conscious, living-in-the-everyday-world woman is not aware of this primitive force within herself. And so it must play out—but unless the mother is clearly pathological, she has *no awareness* that she is doing this, and thus cannot understand it when her son confronts her with her own untenable image, her own unremitting demands. She does not know that she wants her son to relinquish his right to manhood, to move back into her house, to remain dependent upon her, to be the good child. *She absolutely does not know this.*

In her child she has found fulfillment, meaning, and purpose. In the man she becomes aware on some level of her emptiness. She has lost the control of the omnipotent mother, and now she must control by appealing to that part within all men that still craves the affection of a mother, a steady source of approval and love. And she will make him seek it and continue to seek it, and neither he nor she will ever fully understand this interplay.

It is all unconscious, every bit of it. And that's why it goes on, because there is no awareness of it.

So this apparent mystery really forms the seedbed of the *one* crucial task that faces a man in his growing up, in all of his life: the imperative to free himself from the unconscious manipulations of the bad mother, the terrible aspect of his *real* mother. And only then can he be free to function fully as a man, to become a sensitive human being, a husband, lover, and father, and not a dependent "success" wrapped in the trappings of machismo. Only when he frees himself from his own unconscious servitude is he *fit*, is he *able*, to relate both to himself and to women in a meaningful way.

Yet the mother herself is an ambivalent person, ambivalent in her own right, a bundle of mixed feelings in the presence of her son. Because on some level she also asks the question: "What does *he* want from *me*?" And as an adult entering motherhood she must also ask: "What do *I* want of me?" Probably she doesn't know, not really. Motherhood produces a confusion that a woman must work through, cope with in some way. She may fall back on the old, comfortable formulas of her parents, particularly those of her mother, accepting them unquestioningly, totally unaware of the pitfalls. She may learn what to do with her new son on a practical level, but she cannot learn what to *feel*. The feelings come spontaneously, sometimes unwelcome, maybe even shocking. She is prey to the forces of her own bringing-up, her own cultural and parental indoctrination and conditioning. Ambivalence arises from conflicting feelings.

A patient is almost torn apart by ambivalence regarding pregnancy. Should she? Shouldn't she? Since her potential child has no say concerning his birth, she addresses him in a fantasy and they hold a dialogue:

SHE: Would you like to be my baby? Would you like to be born?

HE: You're a nice person and all that, and you seem to mean well, but if I had my choice I'd rather not.

SHE: But why?

HE: What for? To suffer pain, disease, unhappiness? I know there'd be good times and all that, but when you come right down to it, who needs it? Besides, it's not really fair. It's not fair without consulting the child, and that's exactly the thing no one can do, not *really*.

This sets her to musing, and tears spring to her eyes. "We have kids just for ourselves, don't we? We toy with lives that don't even exist, just to make *us* something special, to do what *we're* supposed to. God, people are selfish!"

Her realization does not mean that she will not have a child. Just that she will recognize her ambivalence. This is an extremely powerful kind of exercise, and I know only a few women who have the courage to attempt it.

Mother is ambivalent without awareness and the ambivalence is communicated to her son, and he may well, often does, come to experience this ambivalence as anxiety, as disapproval, even as being unloved. And so the ambivalent mother can surely become the "bad" mother, just *be-*

cause she is ambivalent, just because she is so human. The image, the potentiality, of the "bad" mother is built in.

Ambivalent: the word itself is a pejorative as we have come to use it over time. Allegedly the ambivalent person not only does not know his or her own mind, but the person called ambivalent *cannot be trusted.* We have come to see the ambivalent person as unpredictable, unclear, capricious, and consequently untrustworthy and even emotionally disturbed. We all tend to act as if we were clear about everything; it's the other person who isn't.

And a child, even an infant, will always sense ambivalence as a negative charge, a shock of unwanted current. Children generally deal well only with stark blacks and whites, opposites, definable attitudes. The battered child as well as the apparently well-loved child will overwhelmingly show devotion to the parent who clearly beats him or clearly loves him. The child confronted mainly with ambivalence wants only to get away—which ranges from the childhood withdrawal called autism, to a scattered, even pointless, rebelliousness later in life, to an almost wholesale ambivalence to living itself.

By a brutal and almost heartbreaking paradox and irony, it is that very built-in ambivalence of the mother that the child finds most difficult to tolerate—and as I've suggested, there is a tendency for the son to construe it as negative emotion, as rejection, and to attempt to assimilate the pain and confusion by creating all women in the split image of all-good and all-bad. The focus becomes one-sided: beneath the illusory all-good woman the equally illusory all-bad woman will eventually emerge and seem to overwhelm everything with the force of a tidal wave.

Ambivalence is apparently the normal state of human existence—the way things are. But we adults, exactly like small children, see it as "bad." When Eastern philosophers and Zen masters urge us to "see clearly," they are telling us to eliminate ambivalence.

The conflicts inherent in this condition are easily observed in the mother as she relates to her son. She may be nervous, insecure, anxious about feeding, and this gets communicated to the child through skin and touch; he wakes her during the night and sooner or later she rebels against this voracious, demanding "stranger" and communicates *that* to him while trying not to; she may feel some anxiety about the sight of his genitals and communicates that as well, also while trying not to; or his first steps may mean to her that he is growing up and will soon be separating from her—but how can she admit to this kind of apprehension? Later she may experience a seething anger when her husband begins to make a connection with his growing son, seeing him as a worldly force pulling the boy into adulthood. Or she might fear that she will be forever trapped in a maternal role and become depressed and hostile toward her son for being the cause of the trap.

Always she is coping with anxious, angry feelings, and trying desperately not to have them because by all the standards of society and motherhood she *should not have* negative feelings—and even this may trigger off her anger because if it were not for her son's existence she would not be feeling these things at all, these "bad" feelings that she does not want to have, should not have. And someday she will lose him to another woman—and to some mothers that can be an unbearable anticipation.

Oddly enough, the "good" feelings always seem to be taken for granted, as if only they are givens. But the "bad" feelings become charged with power and force and rage—and as in psychotherapy, his rage must always be experienced first, the negative feelings acknowledged and vented, before a man can ever allow that his mother also provided him with strengths.

And with each perception by the son of his mother's ambivalence, which is felt as negativity, the void opens, the distance spreads between him and his mother, the feeling of being prematurely cut off—and he seeks to avoid this panic by trying to move even closer to her. But what he meets is the ambivalence itself, the mixed feelings, the apparently unaccepting attitudes toward him—and he will always end up asking, "What does she want from me? What does she want from me in order to express pure, unadulterated affection and acceptance?" And now we can see the question in still another sense: "What does she demand of me so that she can make me happy? If only I could find out. If I could find out I'd give it and I'd be happy."

This quest goes on because men *really believe* that she knows. And she refuses to tell—and is, for that very reason, a demon. She must know, because she is the most powerful force on the face of the earth.

Although he might deny it, the man is always searching for happiness, for bliss, for a return to the safety and security of some dimly remembered existence when there was no ambivalence, no pressure, no demands, when he was fed and content—and this perpetual quest has been brutalized by the one myth Freud used in his system, as if it were the only myth alive within the human being, and he distorted its purity to make his point. I mean the oedipal situation, the cornerstone of a psychology invented by a male who needed to play down the dependence on mother (Freud never dealt with true infantile dependence) and paint it sexual, *as if* the boy child had active genital wishes to copulate with his mother.

But this is clearly an adult game: adult men tend to see intimacy with women in genital sexual terms. So men may dream or be surprised by a fantasy of having sexual contact with their mothers—yet what these dreams and fantasies really indicate is that men desperately want to be mothered, they want the contact of mother–child, but adulthood casts it all in sexual terms—and men become properly spooked by it and miss the entire message.

We have no cultural model for this wished-for return to bliss: on the contrary, our culture demands that men abandon the quest because it is regressive and childish—although everyone realizes its drive and impulsion in the wide use of alcohol, drugs, sex, in the headlong pursuit of "happiness." But it is still more manly, and clearly more macho, to be upset by a *genital* situation (intercourse with mother) than a little-boy situation (cuddling with mother). The void that men experience when they feel cut off from their unambivalent "good" mothers they try to fill with genital activity; whereas in the East the void is actively pursued, wherein is experienced the reuniting with mother, the original bliss. In other words, becoming a child again seems to be a bona fide wish and goal of humankind and should not reflect on the quality of a person's manhood.

There is a deep aspect of all men that remains the child, and to say that men should not connect with it, that it can and perhaps should be psychoanalyzed away, is to cripple a vital part of men's emotional lives and obliquely to stress that men must always assume that they have been reared by a "bad" mother. Trying to leave all that behind, men act grown up by chalking up a scorecard of orgasms, all in the service of trying to reunite with the good mother. Everything remains ambivalent.

The ambivalent mother herself: what does she produce

in the ambivalent son? What choice does he have but to latch on to, connect with, the ambivalence itself? What else does he know, what else can he experience? Again, the son attempts to split the ambivalence into good and bad just in order to make sense of it, in order, really, not to go "crazy." And he will search perpetually for the good mother and try to avoid the bad. But here we must ask why the man in the bar (and the majority of his contemporaries) gravitates precisely to a woman who seems so overwhelmingly *bad* for him. The search for the good mother blinds him to the fullness and complexity of his wife's personality; he will have no awareness of the bad side if it is not immediately expressed directly by her behavior. He literally does not see it. "Bad" sides of the personality are rarely expressed in the early days of a love relationship—but these neurotic aspects of the person will eventually surface as the business of daily living begins, when unrealistic expectations play out and fizzle, when woman is fantasized as mother, when man is fantasized as father *or* mother. The man's experience is that he once gravitated toward something good; and who will take bad if good is available? And then he finds himself overwhelmed and he cannot understand it at all.

After seven years of an uncooperative, angry marriage, a friend divorces and wages a three-year campaign of anger against the woman. She remains a bitch, a devourer, a persecutor. She takes him to court for back alimony payments even though he was seriously ill for several months. She is unrelenting, bad-mouths him to friends, excoriates him to their children. Even divorced, nothing softens.

And then he meets another woman, a divorcée. She seems soft, warm, giving. Their sexual experiences are like nothing he imagined even as an adolescent. As time passes, they begin to quarrel. She adores him, she says; she is all love; if only he would understand that, everything would be fine. But he doesn't seem *able* to understand that. He wants to talk and she sees no point in it. He can't sit quietly without her saying, "What's wrong?" If he becomes angry she takes it to imply that he is no longer in love with her. It comes to a point where he can no longer even wash his socks without her experiencing this as a rejection of her love and caring.

She is all love; she is Aphrodite. Why would he want to spend a moment away from her? And he cannot stand it, and leaves her. He feels sucked into the earth, into the sea, confronted by a totally inhuman kind of "love"—the love of utter possession. He runs away literally to save his identity.

Yet he is torn apart and continues to wonder how he could abandon this woman. What did he do wrong?

So here is an aspect of the "bad" mother that is not appreciated at first, or even second, glance: the complete wish to dominate, to turn the man into a child. What looks like an all-giving, unselfish love turns out to be perceived and felt as a domination in which the identity of the man becomes gradually more submerged—where discussions are arguments, where the least shred of individuality is seen by the woman-mother as a pulling away, a lack of love and fidelity.

There is no doubt that this woman is capable of the expression of great warmth and love; friends of the couple see this aspect clearly, and she seems able to express these qualities with an almost superhuman selflessness. But they are also aware that when they talk with her she cannot understand why two husbands have fled from her. She sees no need to explore even the possibility that she herself may have played some negative role in the breakup of her relationships. She continues to hold herself out as the embodiment of perfect love—but what she cannot grasp is that she poisons her own capacity for love, for true adult connection, by remaining in the role of an all-embracing mother who wishes to make boy-children of her men, to render them completely dependent upon her. She is all love, and if they cannot accept this they are, in her words, "very sick, they can't love." She has confused adult love with a maternal embrace. To her, all men are little boys.

Thus she is actually the embodiment of the legendary terrible mother, one aspect of which is to smother her son-lover in her all-consuming embrace. And she has no idea that she is doing this, and consequently has no idea why, with all her lovingness, her relationships are disasters. Most men must flee from this kind of encounter, which, in dreams and fantasies and feelings, is seen as strangulation, smothering, being tied fast with ropes or chains, pinned— a state of servitude to the woman, and ultimately to the mother, the *bad* aspect of the mother. There can be no freedom in this kind of "love" and one must grow up and away from it—or become a caricature of a person.

And yet the attraction a man feels for this kind of "love" is absolutely magnetic. It is soft, dark, totally dependent—for her totally maternal, for him totally infantile. And ultimately destructive.

It's important to understand that we are dealing here with an age-old problem—the eternal interchange between mother and son—and it is necessary to give ourselves a context for it all so that we don't think that we are dealing with some kind of contemporary phenomenon or some trend or phase that will quickly pass. And also so that we don't feel so terribly alone in this matter, helpless and accusatory.

The human race has a long and rich, if at times admittedly strange, heritage. How far back in that history does this image of the "bad" mother run? What forms has it taken, and what solutions have been posed, to remove this burden from mothers, women, boys, and men? And where did it all start?

The "bad" mother—the "terrible" mother of mythology —is a far more complex and mysterious figure than the mother superficially labeled as a poor nurturer, a withholding woman, a punisher, a woman who does not particularly like the role of motherhood—in short a rather nasty, cold person who gives her children little love and comfort.

The bad mother goes back a long way and runs deep in the hidden crevices of our consciousness: she is an aspect of the Indian Kali, the goddess of many arms, the spider, the devourer—an image of many terrifying facets that is reincarnated in dreams and fantasies. She lives inside all men, but too often men haven't the faintest idea that she is there—and from this darkness, from this unconsciousness, the unawareness of her, relationships with mother become excruciatingly painful, marriages become arenas of struggle, relationships with all women frequently teeter on the brink of an emotional hell.

Without a knowledge of this terrible woman within, men project it outward, cast it away, place it within the person of an ordinary human being—an ordinary woman— and then believe they have linked themselves to a demon.

And if the woman with whom a man is linked possesses any characteristics of "badness" in reality, fantasy joins that reality, the woman becomes the spider, and the result is a fall over the brink into the abyss. And the experience is one of annihilation, even the end of all meaning.

A number of psychological theories suggest that all people are *born* with the potentiality of activating these primeval images within—a genetic idea that, espoused most recently by Jung, assumes we are born with the possibility of forming age-old images just as animals are born with a repertory of instincts. It only needs some exposure to the reality of living to give shape and content to this propensity for image-making.

These are sound points. Otherwise, how could the bad or terrible mother assume any of her many ancient frightening forms in dreams and fantasies? How could an ordinary human being, who looks like a woman and can do only what human women do—how could a mere human being assume the appearance of a many-armed Kali, a spider, an octopus, a devouring animal? How could the myths have been transmitted without the persistence through the ages of these images? How could they appear in the dreams of people in and out of psychotherapy? How could they appear in literature, in paintings and sculpture? How, if they do not already exist in some form deep within all of us? The artist may express them directly, but that does not mean that the nonartist does not possess them or is not possessed *by* them.

And they haunt us all.

Part of the key to the bad or terrible mother—and this is familiar in everyday situations—is that she wants, needs, requires, demands *more*. More what? More *than* what? An age-old question that does not seem to have a single answer; a question that has plagued all sons, all men in strife-ridden relationships with wives or lovers. The plaint of the men I have already described.

As I've said, one of the commonest male expressions of despair and frustration, often dismissed as a whine, is: "What does she want—blood?" Or: "She's bleeding me to death."

In 1868 the British Raj made it a crime in India to sac-rifice human beings to the bad-mother aspect of the goddess Kali. But the practice persisted, and quite possibly it may still exist secretly in remote villages.

As men have conceptualized and mythologized her, the goddess, the terrible mother, apparently wants blood, hu-man sacrifice, propitiation. That is what she seems to re-quire in the eyes of the men who must pay her homage, who hear her. Like any mother, she gives all; she gives life. But she can also take it away—and she must be kept satis-fied or her wrath becomes a frenzy of destruction.

Anthropologists tell us this mystique is traced back to a time in human history when cultures turned from hunting to planting—from a way of life that was capricious, insecure, and sporadically violent, to a life made more stable by the cultivation of crops, by the diminished need to follow a nomadic existence in search of food. This shift is tradition-ally seen as marking the time when the masculine image began its steady alteration—the man no longer being the hunter by virtue of physical strength and prowess, but verg-ing toward the priest who would preside over the keeping of the fields and flocks.

And the woman? She began a steady rise in prestige and power, at least symbolically, because her function of giving birth became equated with the fertility of the fields. The fruits of the gods—children, crops—were seen to emanate from a divine womb, and the human woman herself became divine.

But perhaps another kind of event needed to take place before the goddess could be fully formed, before it was decided that she could be wrathful, that she needed propitiation and blood sacrifice. And perhaps that event was the natural disaster: famine, floods, drought, locusts.

And then she became split: the good, bountiful mother was discovered to have a fierce, terrible aspect: a year of life-giving rain followed by a year of crippling drought. And she seemed to need blood, the fluid of life itself.

In an incredible report made by a sea captain several hundred years ago, he told of witnessing a primitive tribal chieftain undergo a ritual which consisted in taking razor-sharp knives and, in full view of the populace, stoically paring away his fingers, ears, toes, until finally, bleeding to death and dismembered as far as one can mutilate oneself, he cut his throat. A picture of primitive man going through an orgy of seasonal propitiation so that the goddess of the earth would continue to give, continue to provide.

We today still live with these images except that they have no means of ritual expression—but they well up in our personal relationships in forms that we are totally unaware of, leaving us in despair and frustration.

What follows through the pages of history is a kind of tragedy, inasmuch as one sort of brutality was substituted for another. Men revolted, subjugated women through brute force and rewritten religious codes, and gained ascendancy. Men had their roles—important, dynamic. Gods became male. And women were forced into their role of submission and weakness and, in some religious systems, depicted as evil and unclean. We don't have to go into the all-familiar history of women being condemned as agents of Satan who by their sexual seductiveness tempt men to everlasting perdition.

Yet the single most important aspect of this entire historical development is that the images inside us have become hidden, not expressed openly and accepted as they once were, but forced deeper and deeper within us until we have become largely unconscious of them. And without awareness of them, they play themselves out to our sorrow and destruction.

The man I spoke of before, the man who fled the seemingly all-loving but ultimately smothering woman: What might he have done had he understood these different aspects of the woman? What might she have done if she had some knowledge of these forces within herself—and knowledge, too, of the way men respond to them? They might then have understood each other and realized that they were living through a situation that has existed for thousands of years. And they might have worked it out. But knowing nothing, they could do nothing except flee, feel hurt, become defensive, and feel demolished.

To understand the power of the forces within us is to change (awareness *is* change), is to see as clearly as we are capable of seeing. Otherwise the pain goes on, unremittingly.

Having these forces and images driven deep into us has led directly to the false elevation of real women into powerful goddesses; and has turned men into creatures who must get away at all costs. And the need both to examine this relationship and take knowledge from it has resulted in the emergence of another mythic figure which, as we will see, is still alive within men but fails to find adequate expression except through some internal search.

This is a myth common to every culture that has ever

left us a heritage: the myth of the hero. It is a myth that has often been taken as merely a story, sometimes a tale of high adventure, sometimes a cautionary parable—depending on the art or intent of the recorders. It is the story of Jonah and the Whale, of Parsifal, of the Celtic Oisin, of Gilgamesh and Osiris, of Jesus Christ, and of hundreds of lesser figures, all of whose lives reflect the necessity of emerging from the darkness into the light of awareness.

This is the same life-giving myth that, if worked through and made real, made pertinent to life today as it surely is and must be, is the factor above all else that eventually leads to cure in psychotherapy, to consciousness in other disciplines aimed at the liberation of the human being. Psychotherapy may help with problem-solving; communication may improve; a bit of pain may vanish; whatever. But there is no cure, no road to cure, to meaning, to life, without the journey of the hero—and that journey involves immersion into the darkness in order to emerge into light. And the problem—and I feel this is especially true for men —is that men wish to achieve light without the journey into darkness. And they usually attempt this via the intellect— through facts, knowledge, logic; and if they are not intellectual, then with their fists. Power of some sort. But it never works: the intellect fails before the soft drawing-in of the darkness, brutality leads only to more brutality—and the unconscious, the beckoning, devouring mother, will win at last.

Jonah was swallowed by a whale—by his unconscious, by the world-mother trying to draw him back inside and make of him a dependent, helpless man. He enters her, then forcibly leaves her. In some similar myths, this exit is accomplished by cutting through, or by the lighting of the fires of consciousness. But the journey inward must be made *before* the journey outward into the real life of the world.

What more can these ancient stories, still buried deep within us, tell us about the bond between mother and son?

Oisin, the Celtic almost-hero, journeys into the underworld, then crosses the boundary into a new world. His inner guide tells him that he must never turn back, must never return to the land from which he emerged—that he must be independent and free. Because there is no second chance. And yet he turns back. He returns, admonished that if he must do so he must protect himself by not touching the land, the earth (and the earth is *always* mother). And by accident, by carelessness, *without consciousness,* he does touch the earth and suddenly becomes old, suddenly becomes blind. The ageless youth of his inner life, his light, is quenched; he can no longer see within. And in his sudden old age he is again like a dependent, unconscious infant.

And Parsifal, like all the knights of the Grail, must set out on the journey to consciousness, to awareness, to independence. And their symbol was not merely the Grail which unites all personal fragments into a healing whole; the symbolic quest begins always with the knight entering a part of the deep forest (again the mother, again the unconscious) through a path never before taken—the personal search aimed at a universal goal. One must reunite with the mother as a man, not a child.

And even Jesus Christ—the son, the man, whose spiritual and life-giving message was barely rescued from the myth that began to grow around his mother. Until finally the church forbade the forming of Virgin cults. As a mother, she may intercede with her son, but she must not be worshipped as a deity.

And the Jews? There is no room for anyone but Yahweh, the all-masculine god, and that can only be an in-credibly brutal reaction against the image of the bad mother. In traditional Judaism the woman remains a second-class citizen.

And so it has been and so it goes—the constant, blatant, deeply ingrained fear and hatred of the image of the bad, terrible, controlling mother whose role is to prevent the growth of male consciousness and independence, and se-duce, entice, her son back into the all-encompassing mater-nal embrace.

How this all began, how it all happened precisely, is lost in the mysteries of prehistory—but the images persist, re-emerging repeatedly through all the epochs of history and literature—and the psychic struggle with the bad mother *is acted out every day in every corner of the world* with the same power as the myths themselves.

Men continue to live out the myth of the terrible mother, and it is because they will not look into it, will not free themselves from it, that they remain on a profound level little more than children in many aspects of their lives —and it is also because of their refusal to enter the thick forests of unconsciousness that they continue to cast the mother in this poisonous role.

Could it be that part of the reason for this refusal to look is a need to blame *her* for what men cannot accom-plish? Or are they truly afraid to lose her? We shall see.

Obviously men have tried to leave the bad mother, or at least the inner image of her, by marrying—and yet, more often than not, marrying the bad mother herself, the image hidden beneath an exterior that dazzles men with some ap-parent "difference"—something seductive, something that blinds sight.

There was the tragic and poignant story of John Balt (a

pseudonym), who some years ago wrote a book called *By Reason of Insanity*. He killed his wife, violently carving her to pieces with a kitchen knife after she had been browbeating him at a time of intense stress for him. So he killed her. And found out only later during a highly successful treatment in prison that he killed her because *at that moment* he did not know who she was. Or rather saw in her only the image of his mother, who had constantly threatened him with abandonment to an orphanage when he was a child.

He killed his mother in a mythic struggle to be free, to avoid being swallowed by the image of the terrible mother— and unlike Attis, who castrated himself to appease his mother, Cybele, he hacked his mother to pieces.

But by reason of insanity he killed a real woman, and with that killing destroyed what he loved.

Perhaps Dostoevski said it all in the first page of *Crime and Punishment* when Raskolnikov, after reading a destructive letter sent by his mother, takes his axe and shortly afterward murders an old lady who is just enough like his mother to spur the myth into action, to blind him to the reality of what stood before him. And so she died.

And like all men, he suffers the guilt for having killed, for wanting to kill, his mother in her terrible aspect.

These are powerful images, powerful forces, and they live on within us waiting to spring forth, given the proper timing, as they *have been* acted out by men in mental hospitals and on death rows. They are too powerful to be shrugged off; they can be lightened by the humor of jokes, but they can never be exorcised until they are faced individually within us. Only after this confrontation is experienced can that latent murderousness be expunged—and men will finally be able to see the women who stand before them as the people they truly are, not as living embodiments of primitive mythology.

The truly pathological aspects of the mother-son relationship will interest us to some degree because there are bad mothers who are bad because they are brutally damaged emotionally, and from this well of sickness they impart sickness to their sons. Such mothers are easily observed: again, we can see them on video tapes feeding their infants without real contact or engagement, dangling them from their laps or hands like so many rag dolls, schizophrenia in the making; I have even seen one such damaged mother let her baby slip and fall, then stare blankly as if a cocktail napkin had slipped from her lap. And there are battered children, brutally beaten and brought to hospital emergency rooms because of a "fall" resulting in black eyes, broken cheekbones, fractured arms.

But these are blatant affairs, and the damage inflicted is direct, deadly—and such children are lucky indeed if they make it at all. Let's turn to more subtle stuff, and a good image that binds much of what I've talked about so far is the male transvestite—which, by the way, is a much more common phenomenon than many people would suspect. I am not talking only about the man who walks openly through the streets dressed in women's clothing, but the many men who keep a small cache of panties and bras and every now and then put them on in the privacy of their own homes.

The meaning of this behavior will become clear in a moment.

Frequently these men are highly successful in the world: little problem with earning money, promotions at jobs, and frequently very little trouble in attracting women. Essentially they are heterosexual—but they are inextricably tied to their mothers and must return to an experience which brings them closer to the mother than overt dependency on a woman. That is, they dress in female clothing as a way of getting back into the mother's flesh—surrounding themselves with intimate garments, with the experience being all the more intense if the underwear has actually been worn by a woman, even more gratifying if her smells remain.

What is being expressed here?

Something profoundly poignant.

On the one hand, dressing in women's clothing is a way of alleviating the terrific anxiety these men feel because of the pressures of having to act like stereotyped males in our society. Quite simply, on this level, they are returning to mother to obtain relief from the struggles of daily living that they regard at times as overwhelming. And if the dressing is followed by masturbation—which it frequently is—it is difficult to tell whether anything truly sexual was experienced in the dressing or whether the man uses masturbation to get in touch with his own male sexuality as a way of emerging from the belly of the whale, from the darkness of the unconsciousness into which he has plunged himself for some brief time. Because in donning his "mother's" clothing he has, like Attis, castrated himself and become a nonsexual boy child; and when the gratification from this has been absorbed, he must reemerge into the world, restitute the function of his penis—or stay where he is and become lost.

Mythically, again, there have been many rituals in which men have dressed in women's clothing, and this has been symbolic of the propitiation of the earth mother, the return to the womb, to the chaos of unconsciousness.

The image of the "bad mother" that lurks within this context is obviously not a brute, a child-beater, whatever—but the image of the mother who has never allowed her son to take his independence, to move away in any meaningful manner, and who has been buttressed in her almost demonic possessiveness by the father who for his own reasons of abject dependency has never tried to separate mother from boy or to provide an active model of maleness.

But what is the son returning to when he dresses in women's clothes? Certainly not a mother who destroys him, but simply a "good" mother who once, very early, provided him with the only true place of "safety" in the world—within her, close to her. And more often than not, the ordinary man cannot find this in a mate or a lover; instead he must confront a real woman—an independent woman and not a mother. And so he must find some other way to effect his reentry into the dark security of her body.

He may do it through transvestism, or on an apparently less unacceptable and *less imperative and needy* level, through drugs or alcohol—through drug- or liquor-induced feelings of oneness, of oceanic bliss, of a feeling of an entire absence of anxiety and tension. He may do it through a quest for the bliss of meditation, where all personal problems and attachments are to be lost in the pure cosmic consciousness and connection with the All. But this too is an illusion, certainly as futile as drug-induced illusions—because what is being avoided is the look within. And by trying to avoid the needed journey into full life, which necessitates the leaving of mother behind and union with a real woman, he seeks to plunge into the mother by calling it something else: *samadhi, satori, nirvana.*

But he can call it what he will. What he is looking for is his mother. And his approach can be high-chic, a status symbol. He meditates, he is in touch. In truth he sits and thinks, but instead of dealing with what is inside him, he attempts to submerge his chaos and dependency in mysticism, seeking far outside of him what he cannot face within.

Here the "bad" mother is the mother from whom the man cannot free himself, the mother he cannot truly face, cannot confront and emerge whole—and as the transvestite would rather think that his wearing women's panties is a sexual turn-on and not the falling back into the womb that it is, the pseudo mystic would rather think that he is seeking a higher *objective* connection than bliss at the breast or in the womb of his mother.

This kind of "bad" mother is the mother we have all had the most familiarity with, the kind of mother that exists within all of us, neither a murderer nor a beast—but a woman who, from her own needs to cling to what she sees as the man within, attempts *without any awareness whatever* to mold her boy child into the man of her dreams.

But he cannot be both her man and her boy, and he ends up not necessarily "sick," but in some state of debilitation, making it all the more difficult to shed the crippled boy and emerge into manhood. And the mother will be consciously felt and described as "bad" only later when his attempts at showing her his manhood get rebuffed.

FOUR

THE SAFE MOTHER AND THE UNSAFE MOTHER

Now, can the portrait of the "good" mother be any less complex than the portrait of the "bad" mother? Certainly both the good and the bad mother exist in the total person, whom I have already described as basically ambivalent, each emerging with a kind of capriciousness at times, a form existing for each of them within all men. To say that the good is merely the flip side of the bad is to miss the point entirely. As we will see, goodness, as well as badness, is many-faceted.

What have we come to think of as the good mother? Is it simply that she doesn't act or think like some of the mothers I've sketched in the last chapter? Is she merely a wholesome, loving, self-sacrificing person—a remnant in modern dress of the sweet, knowing, vaguely martyred gray-haired heroines of movies of the 1930s? Is she even the sweet, harried, often beaming lady who coos in television ads about the quality of one diaper over another, who thrills to her gleaming waxed floor, who seems almost spaced on love as her children eat their instant soups at lunchtime?

Or are we again, because of our cultural obsession with opposites (God-Satan, black-white, good-bad), to be forced into a definition by default, gauging the "good" by the absence of "bad"?

Consider for a moment that we find it far simpler—perhaps even oddly "natural" as a result of our educations—to define some quality, some essence, some state of being, by focusing on its opposite. This approach is inescapable in our culture; it exists in this book. Put another way, whenever we seek to capture something good or wholesome or natural, we first consider the deviations from it. That has been the story of the psychiatric wrestling match with the "normal" personality; it remains rather loosely defined, even mysterious, safer to talk about in the form of graphs, charts, and averages and norms. The "psychopathology" (the "badness") of a person is, to some minds, much clearer to see and grasp (though even this person will elicit different diagnoses from different therapists). It can be fairly safe to say that the study of, and ultimate definitions of, the human personality began in the bedrock of "pathology" and continues to be expressed in these terms. We can "see" that a person is depressed; that he or she is trembling with anxiety; that a particular person is lost in a hallucination; that a murderer has killed someone while being detached from what we term reality. These we can see; and we make efforts to hook any piece of psychopathology to its alleged roots somewhere in the bringing-up process. We claim to see the truth in this; we think we can see more and infer more from a life that has gone wrong. We almost never know what it is that has gone *right* except through the absence of "psychopathology" or symptoms.

The same has held true of mothering. The bad mother seems easy to spot most of the time; her effects are felt keenly and painfully—and there are theories of personality that lay all psychopathology squarely at the feet of the mother, giving rise, for example, to such terms as the "schizophrenogenic mother," a mother who has "made" her child schizophrenic. The field is becoming a bit more sophisticated of late, but the prejudice against the mother remains, for we cannot avoid the fact that it is, after all, the mother who has the greatest impact upon her child from the moment of birth.

This is a hard pill to swallow for most mothers: they stand accused by the psychiatric inventors of pathology words, but somehow they never receive credit for what they have done right. Because no one really knows what has gone right. Except that the child is not overtly mad and does what most of his peers do.

We look in the wrong direction for what has gone right. "Right" requires a new and perhaps even startling definition.

A successful male writer and rebel with an unerring eye for social "games" and superficial life-styles bemoans:

Whenever I think of my mother I get enraged. There isn't a thing she doesn't know about or a thing she doesn't criticize. She swallowed me up when I was a child and she won't let go. I show her a story and she whips out some piece of silly poetry she's written. One day she's a demon, the next day she tries to seduce me into her life—and when I bite at the bait she clobbers me. There isn't a time I can remember when she hasn't somehow pulled the rug out from under me: totally capricious. Reality has no meaning to her, it really doesn't. She can look at a bald fact and shrug her shoulders—and I swear to God it's like she invents the world every day. She's cracked, completely cracked, completely hysterical.

When asked if he would change his life right now, trade his talent and rebelliousness and his fits of depression (which he has periodically) for another kind of life, he says, "I could do without the depression, and I could do without the anger—but no, overall I wouldn't trade off."

But *can* he have the talent without the anger and depression? What prevents this man from seeing what his mother *gave* him? What stops him from understanding that her drama has helped him develop his own drama, that her capriciousness has allowed him to see into the capricious madness of the world in which he lives, that her manipulation of "reality" has in some way contributed to *his* manipulation of it in his stories and novels, that in some way she has helped to show him that there are different ways of looking at the world—in short, that she has helped him release a vast array of inner images that he brings to his vision of life and art?

Why can't he give her credit for helping him to forge a way of being in the world that he himself says he would not give up or trade? Perhaps it is his grandiosity: perhaps he won't give her credit because he feels that it will somehow detract from his accomplishments, that they will be hers and not his. Or perhaps the answer lies in his bitter comment that he could do without his depression and anger—both of which are integral pieces in his existence. Perhaps, like most of us, he hates and fears pain. And perhaps there are many more reasons and nonreasons. But the fact remains that, like many men, he somehow cannot really give her credit for anything, can only condemn her for what he feels she has done badly.

It is in the configurations of a personal life like this one that we might best search for the "good" mother.

It is one of the axioms of psychotherapy that most men are angry if they are doing what their mothers want them to do. They feel like puppets. But one day, after the anger abates, they begin to feel at peace with themselves when it seems acceptable that they do something that runs in tandem with the wishes of their mothers.

And it is also a truism, at least to sensitive therapists, that *somewhere* in the almost fathomless complexity called the mother–son relationship there is a force for good, for strength, for meaning, for an urge into life. But to men this force is invisible, so preoccupied and bitter are they that anything at all has gone wrong, that they can be depressed or pained or anxious, that the mother has nudged them out of the nest into a world in which they must make their own way. The son resents the loss of bliss, and he resents mother for letting him go even to the degree that she has—and she *has*; to some degree she lets her son go even though it often seems that she wishes to hold him, control him, dominate him.

She is resented, raged at, because she has "caused" her son's bouts of depression (which bring him close to insight if only he would see it), "caused" his anxiety (which also tells us all something about being alive in the world), "caused" ... well, the list is apparently endless.

But by giving pain she opens the realities of the world.

There is resentment in being thrown into the world, and

it is as if she will never be forgiven for doing that part of her job that she *must* do unless she is an emotional cripple. Even when a mother tries to dominate her son she is giving him an opportunity to rebel against her and consequently to find his own path, to discover independence; when she tells him what is right and wrong, the opportunity is there for him to one day reach his own conclusions; and even when she may try to castrate him emotionally, he has the opportunity to say "No, you can't do that" and bring his penis into erection to defy her. Even then the mother is casting her son into the world with the message that life is filled with pain and suffering and that they must be experienced and accepted along with pleasure and joy.

I will return to this in a moment, but it should be said here that the search for the good mother in the wrong direction has produced an incredible amount of confusion. But it has also led to a statement by the late British psychotherapist D. W. Winnicott that brought a sigh of relief from all interested parties: Winnicott coined the phrase "good-enough mothering."

But no one can really know what that means. Good enough for what? The answer here seems to be, when the phrase is cut to the bone, that the child does not, during growth and in adulthood, display a significant amount of debilitating symptoms. I want to be entirely fair to Winnicott because he was a brilliantly sensitive and feeling man who contributed immeasurably to the field of mental health —but we are still struck by the basic fact that his phrase is nevertheless, though not with black-and-white contrast, describing something by the absence of something else.

Is the successful man, the good family man, the good husband and provider, whatever—is this man the product of good-enough mothering? Hard to know. Perhaps he is; or perhaps his secret life is a freak-out. Who knows, as long as he appears socially "normal"—i.e., does, like a child, what his peers do? Is the ability to trust, the capacity to love, the recognition of one's own "craziness," the man who recognizes that on some level he is playing a strange social game, the man who recognizes in himself a being larger than the small figure of the typical male: are these factors more than the results of good-enough mothering?

Let's break this package down. There is little doubt that a lot of "good" mothering has forged the character of the man who can make a satisfactory marriage and to some degree accept that in his mate he can have both mother and lover. And that he doesn't (again a definition based on a negative) live in a state of general deprivation, always wanting something he can't get, is another indication that mother has not gone awry. That he can feel love without always questioning the motives of his lover is still another sign. And we can go on and on.

But notice that most of these traits, these characteristics, exist purely on a level that allows him to be not terribly pained in waking life, and that they only imply something sound in the inner life, the life of dreams and images and propulsions. And that is all right, not to be criticized, because what most of us are vitally concerned with is the daily life in the world—the going to work, making love, enjoying the children; these are goals, ends, socially desired ways of thinking, feeling, and behaving. We are very concerned with "good" behavior and social approbation: we very much want to fit in, to be "normal," to be, in essence, a happy, non-boat-rocking member of a small social world that fits into a larger social world.

This man may be the product of good-enough mothering, but is it *good* mothering? It is good-enough only because he can be defined by his neighbors, and perhaps to some degree by himself, as living up to a *hoped-for* social norm. The go-getter, the breadwinner, the man who plans his investments soundly, who is seen tossing footballs with his son, taking his daughter to puppet shows, mowing his lawn, paying visits to his parents, perhaps contributing as much as he can to his local church—all these traits would certainly be described as the results of good mothering.

And they are, *on that level of existence*—on the level of moving from one small family to a larger social family.

Yet by altering the phrase, let us assume that the traits exhibited by this man are *not* products of good mothering. *They are products of safe mothering.* And the keystone is *security.*

The world described above is a world of *ostensible* safety. It is a defined world which turns on the adequate performance of roles—or, if you will, a variety of what we call *selves.* It seems consistent, thus giving the illusion of wholeness, purpose, meaning. It is a world in which everything seems to go right as long as the role is played fervently: it is a world society craves. And as long as the structure remains safe, cohesive, held together by something or other we cannot define—but which usually is money or what appears to be cooperation by spouses and neighbors in mutual goals—the world may well adhere, and the mothering that helped produce it seems indeed good enough—on that level. But more, it is *safe:* it is a product of safe mothering in which no chances can be taken, and where pain, depression, and agony can have no place.

Yet if it is so safe, why then can the structure so easily fall apart?

After *his* world falls apart, a patient says:

How can fifteen years go down the drain so fast? I lose my job, have trouble finding another one, the bank makes a little trouble, and now suddenly everybody's drinking. Everybody's afraid we're going to have to move to some shack, my kids look at me like I'm a murderer, my wife's in a panic. It's like there's nothing to keep us from each other's throats. What the hell is going on? Don't we have anything meaningful inside of us to pull us through? It's like four walls with emptiness inside.

While of course a number of people can weather events like this, a great, great many can't and don't. And that is the problem with safe mothering: it requires safe arms later in life, and when the arms of society are withdrawn the child falls. Very often you can see how many men have fallen by peering behind the "For Sale" signs posted on suburban lawns: a few are "moving up," more are divorcing, many are crumbling.

And they are *not* sick, not "psychopathological," not damaged. Their "good-enough mothering" has, metaphorically, reached the limits of its good-enoughness, and the pain of abandonment by the system, the pain of recognition that comes with the discovery that the people we seem to have let down are somehow different from the people who once shared our illusory safety—*that* event produces a dumb, numbing anguish that we cannot understand.

Mother cannot be blamed, although she will be, as surely as water falls when it rains. Mother cannot really be blamed because in giving an illusion of "safety," of security, she has done a job she herself has been conditioned to do—and it is not her fault if her son does not take the opportunity to inquire into his assumptions, into his life, does not question his existence, is lulled into a life purely on the *surface* of the earth.

If safe or good-enough mothering has not magically transmitted a sense of great depth, great resources, then men must find them for themselves. What other task is there?

But does the idea of a "safe" mother imply a mother who is "unsafe"? If so, what happens that is different?

First I want to make the flat statement that there is some degree of damage inherent in all mothering. No woman can mother a son perfectly; no person knows that much, nor is any mother entirely free of her human problems. Some recognition of this maternal imperfection led in the past to all sorts of "scientific" regimens, such as schedule feeding and rigid toilet training, and perhaps even shows through in the current emphasis on "having" to breast-feed —another form of rigidity. In the Western world we are dazzled by the apparent ability of technology to obliterate human error, forgetting that people themselves invent the paradigms and program the machines.

In the imperfection of human contact there must arise human damage in the mother–child relationship—and the damage runs along a continuum of unrest and disturbance, producing conditions from quirkiness to neurosis to creativity (which may often be coupled with quirkiness or neurosis) to overt psychosis. The points on the continuum are not discrete; they blend, fuse, blur, and what this damage produces is the crucial matter.

Now there are certainly mothers who will reveal to their sons the *potentiality* of discovering their depths without overly damaging them. They are strange ones, these mothers, because they offer possibilities for looking at and experiencing life that are breathtaking in scope. They give their sons not only a vision of maternal bliss, but a profound vision of terror and pain. And in that way, though they may be called crazy by their own sons, they have offered a more balanced vision of what it is to be alive: the soaring pleasures and the abject miseries. And they stir up potentialities for creativity and imagination and no easy acceptance of the status quo, no easy quest for "normality" —in essence communicating that life is made up of earth and fire and water and air. They encourage their sons to fly. They may act as if they wish to ground their sons, to keep them leashed—but in that very posture they encourage the desire and necessity to fly.

The grounded flyer pines for flight, demands flight, *will* fly like the mythic gods. And he knows what it is to fall as well.

Behind the social facade, the normality we all crave, could the good mother really be the mother who stimulates, encourages flight? Flight into the imagination, flight into possibilities, flight to the point where all systems are inadequate, all social norms are suspect—where flight takes one into the many corners of unexplored existence, into individuality and differentiation and true manhood?

Could this crazy, *unsafe* mother, a mother with a vision of both heaven and hell—could this prodding, poking, demanding, covetous, capricious mother be *truly* the good mother?

If so, then this is the mother we are looking for. And I submit that within almost every mother by nature and by a reaction to the oppression of her role, there is a sufficient amount of this wildness and brilliant perversity to allow her son to fly, to imagine, to be different, to take chances, to suffer, to follow the path of his pain, to be fully alive. To become a man.

There is a kind of grandiosity in the unsafe mother, a standing above the rules of society, of authority, that is generally hidden from public view. But it will slip through every so often in a powerful and dramatic way—and then one sees that it has always been there, silently working its way into the fabric of the son's life.

Consider the recollection of a man who during World War II, at the age of ten, experienced a moment of total amazement, almost stupefaction. His mother had had enough of all of it, with the rules, with authority: her husband had been drafted at the age of thirty-eight and she had written a vitriolic letter to President Roosevelt; a butcher in the local supermarket had stolen a page of food-rationing stamps; her promised coal delivery had been postponed because it was not "essential"; her small salary could not be raised due to a wage freeze.

This is the context of what remains one of the strongest and most vivid memories in this man's life:

> My mother and I were attending Mass one Sunday, and after the priest gave his sermon we were asked to stand and take the pledge of the Legion of Decency —an organization that screened movies and plays. We were told to raise our right hands and swear that we would not see movies classed as objectionable or "condemned" by the church. So I stood automatically, raised my hand, and in this absolutely wild moment, in full view of the whole congregation, my mother yanked down my hand and almost growled, "No one's going to tell you what movies you can see." I

was terrified, people were looking at us, but she stood there, defiant and angry—and I just took that strength from her and it was all right being stared at. After all these years, it's still hard to believe it really happened.

This woman is certainly an unsafe mother. She conveys to her son a kind of wildness, rebellion, independence. She turns the world upside down for him—and gives him some sense of himself that later on in life some people might call grandiose or arrogant. She tells him that it is all right to stand above, to be special. *With her permission.*

And this man remains in a relationship to the authority of his mother—and so he may come to see both the justice of authority and its oppressiveness.

One positive aspect—and a powerful one—of what this boy learned early was that he could take a chance, he could defy rote social rules; and the defiance, the chance taking, has led to the formation of a personal ethic, a personal code of values that embraces some social aspects and rejects others that are subscribed to without thought. His mother activated what Hemingway once called a "shit-detector."

The man concludes, as he nears fifty:

Sure, I had to try to work out my problems with her as the ultimate authority, the ultimate force in my life, but I wouldn't have had it any other way, not really. You see, she gave me possibilities, she—how can I say this to get it across—she just about *forced* me to be different and drove me back on my life inside. I had something inside, you see. Some kind of power. So when she activated it, she activated it not only against the authority she hated—but, and this had to be, ultimately against the authority of herself.

She made me dream. It doesn't matter that now she would like me to be a pillar of the community. Actually she's objected to just about everything I've ever done—my wife who's not Catholic, me who's no longer Catholic—how could I be after she worked the church over that morning? You know, when I told her that I was grateful for what she did for me, she just didn't understand.

No problems in being different, "special"?

Plenty of problems. For a time I was a mama's boy, the kids didn't like me, and overall I've been in touch with a tremendous amount of pain. But that's the beauty of the whole damned business—really the beauty of it. She showed me that life could be very painful, there were no easy ways out, I had to create my own rules, my own life. She opened me to the pain of being different, of being rejected for who I was, and I've struggled with it all my life.

But I'll tell you one thing: when I'm sixty-five, and that's just fifteen years away, I won't be hit by sudden shocks. I won't be suddenly pained by social rejection, forced retirement, feeling washed up and useless. I've been there, many times, I know all about it, and it made me somehow a bit old before my time. My sense is that I'll die exactly the way I've lived— being angry or outraged by something, or even happy. But it won't be in a state of numbness or shock.

You know what that woman really did for me? She not only taught me the incredible pain that would come by living my own life—but when I die I'll die feeling that I'm still growing up. The man and the

boy in me—they're always together inside me, alive
... the old man and the young boy.

So obviously there is a sharp difference between the
mother I was beginning to describe above and the mother
that we can call "good enough" in a very straight *social*
sense—between the mother who provides an impetus for
flying and creativity (and hence she will have some "bad"
aspects as well) and the mother who provides a secure background—an, if you will, mundane or "wholesome" bringing-
up. This is the mother who, with minimal obvious problems, likes her infant son, likes many of the various periods
of his chronological growth, does not make efforts to
smother or dominate him, and to a certain extent allows his
father to have a hand in his bringing-up. Usually a "masculine" hand, of getting more involved with the boy when he
becomes a bit more grown up and less dependent on the
world of a nurturing woman. Little League, Saturday car-
pentering, and the rest of it.

Such a boy will probably grow up with some sense of
independence, make his major strides in terms of achievement—good grades, a more or less refined vision of a career
at an early age, a marriage that for a time provides more
comfort than not; in short, a specialist in middle-class life,
goals, and aspirations.

As I mentioned before, this is a life that for a long
while may be relatively free of the great American fear, i.e.,
the fear of pain, suffering, the wrenching of the soul—or, in
clinical terms, depression, the great destroyer of the middle-
class dream. To us, depression equals "bad," which in turn
has its roots in the idea of sin. And for a time the man's
life may be relatively free of anxiety and profound feelings
of inferiority or low self-esteem.

In other words, this kind of mothering molds a social being who accepts society almost blindly because there has never been a reason not to.

But something happens. And that something usually happens around midlife. The event usually gets resolved in essentially two ways, although these ways have many embellishments.

When the inevitable (and it *is* just about inevitable) depression or crash descends on a man who is somewhere around forty—a depression that at first strikes him like a blow, inexplicable, confusing, but actually underpinned by a profound discontent that may emerge when looked at, or may stay submerged and increase the pain and confusion—two things may occur. There is an immediate drive to end the pain. Perhaps he is under stress at his job. A trip to the local physician will produce a prescription for Valium or some other soporific, a sleeping pill. Perhaps there will be a slight increase in "social drinking." And the man muddles through; but eventually he feels himself losing his tenuous grip and falls into a sort of apathy. But he accepts his lot, stays close to his family, friends, and job—and is considered until the day of his retirement a solid citizen. He may even, probably has, woven a value system around his life and work, and rationalizes the pressures and depression by an adherence to the dogma that "this is life." Because of the Valium and his martini the depression and anxiety will diminish, but there will be a nagging within that needs to have the edge blunted by increasing work, by a drive toward living better in the external world, enhancing his life-style, acquiring more possessions—in short, an increase in the activity of trying to find more gratification in the very world that is turning sour. A long time may pass before this behavior comes to a dead end; but it comes sooner these days than it used to just because of the fact that the life span is lengthening and a man becomes more aware of his work and love life grinding to a halt, his overall potency diminishing, his increased notice of ads in the Sunday supplements showing "senior citizens" holding golf clubs on lush Florida greens or sipping tall colorful drinks on "retirement home" patios.

The need for finding external gratification will often take the form of wishing for a young woman to give the illusion of male attractiveness and youth. But aside from perhaps one or two sexual or almost-sexual forays over forty or so years, a man in this position usually manages to control these appetites, weighs a fling against the meaning of his marriage—and calls a halt. The ads keep beckoning to the nirvana of Golden Age Villa—and he has no choice but to go on with it, get there, and have done with it.

Since this is the way it generally goes—on close examination the plotted course of a man's life is almost intolerable in its deadliness of direction—we will have to bring up the question of social norms and values, and come to an observation based on behavioral evidence. The "normality" in this procession of behaviors, its process, goals, and ends, must result from a by-and-large good-enough or at least common-enough mothering experience. One has received the equipment in the "safe" mothering experience to keep on going, keep on moving, seeming to accept the way the society moves, shapes, and pushes—and to come through it without getting *visibly* mangled or destroyed. The internal destruction, though, may be enormous: the destruction of individuality, of freedom and creativity, which leads to a later-life feeling of profound regret and despair—the "normal" problems of advanced middle and old age.

This kind of mothering may be valuable as a crucial underpinning for the fluid movement of the social machine because it keeps the cogs moving, working, retiring, and dying appropriately. This mother, like most therapists, is a social engineer.

The kind of man I've described rarely consults any sort of therapist, always pulls his weight, is often admired for his stability, and can in no way be labeled pathological, sick, or even neurotic. He does his job. He may be viewed sociologically as one blur in a mass phenomenon—the Man in the Gray Flannel Suit, the Organization Man—and his tribulations and pressures dealt with as a social expectation or even a social malaise. But *individually* he is never diagnosed. Except as "normal."

He is, of course, the normal model, consciously or not, for most mental-health practitioners. Because he has an intact ego. He can keep relatively controlled, is not overtly self-destructive, preserves and clings to his social support groups like family and friends, and never loses sight of some sort of plan—some hope that another project, another grasp at the world, will improve his position in it. He *accepts* it all as the norm, the ostensible logic of it all, and does not rebel against the forces at large, because the ego, the consciousness, the reality testing, tells him that a rebellion cannot be won, cannot be effective, and that if he tries he will be *acting out*.

Now look at the sleight of hand. If a man who finds himself in the situation I've been describing catches on to something inside himself, is dimly aware that something is really wrong with his life *internally* and his life *externally*, and turns up at a therapist's office, the therapist immediately goes into this man's background, his "history," and emerges with the inescapable conclusion that something has gone wrong in the mothering (and secondarily, fathering) experience. The man is "depressed," and if his depression is not "reactive," that is, caused by a literal roof falling in, the death of a spouse or child, or loss of a job, then he is depressed because his mothering experience has not been adequate to develop his ego and his sense of self-reliance.

This is often psychiatric claptrap. Not only that, it is demeaning. And finally it is an illusion, and the therapy will often be geared to getting a better performance out of the man—therapists call this "functioning"—while along the way the man must keenly feel the guilt of his nonperformance. But what he is really meant to feel is his guilt over seeing through something—of seeing past the surface to the discord beneath. It is a social rule that *no one* must see— and in his cry of pain, outrage, and anxiety, this man, without even being able to conceptualize it, *sees through it.*

And it is claptrap because the mental-health community, along with the lay community, will define the quality of a man's mothering by whether he seeks out or does not seek out a therapist. *It is that black and white.*

Now, I submit that on a scale of values—totally hypothetical, of course, because such things can't be quantified— the man who seeks help because he is *seeing through something,* because he recognizes that his inner and outer lives are being shaken to their roots, *is the man who has had a better mothering experience.* Not the man who accepts all, does what he is supposed to, and would be still confused by his pain in his coffin if he had the consciousness to feel it.

To be able to question the norms, to selectively reject them, is to have had a *meaningful and potent relationship with a mother,* filled with pain, joy, happiness, misery, love, hate. And anger.

Because to feel the anger is to be able to separate not only from the dependency on the mother but from the ills of society as well.

A fortyish man in a therapy session says:

"I had this dream in which my mother was criticizing everything I did—picking on me, harping on me. In waking life she's critical and I know she has her faults, but she was relentless in the dream, almost like a caricature. She just came at me, over and over. I know I can be a little angry at her, but it makes me feel bad to be angry. She hasn't had a good life, at least not for a lot of years at the beginning, it's been hard for her, and I don't like to feel angry toward her. It's not right. *She always meant the best for me.*"

The therapist replies, "How do you know that?"

And the process of anger begins—and later gets somewhat resolved, not because his mother has been deliberately vicious to him, but because he sees that, like all human beings, she did not always mean the best for him. She often meant the best for herself. But now his anger has let him see it. And in some way, by meaning the best for herself, she gave him enough pain to free himself.

So what I am saying is that the mother—and always remember that I am not talking about the psychotic or near-psychotic mother whose destructiveness is completely obvious—who provides some pain and sorrow and hopelessness along with emotional nourishment may after all be the good mother because she prepares her son to confront the world as it is, as a very mixed place with all its joys and sorrows. This, I believe, is how it happens: by itself, *inherently* played out in the course of this kind of mothering.

It *cannot be planned consciously* because the subtleties of the inner mesh between the psyches of mother and son cannot be translated into a behavioral program. Such an attempt could only result in the *deliberate* infliction of pain, giving the son only the feeling that he is hated, aggressed against, punished.

Conversely, the traditional mother, who has unreflectively been called the good mother—a one-sided woman, all goodness, which religion and society are almost demonically driven to maintain in an untenable and inhuman position— does little more than equip her son to be a social paragon, to adopt an endless variety of roles. The Good Provider, the Successful Husband, the Responsible Citizen, the Man in the World, ad infinitum, are all roles, each of them pinned to the needs of whoever rules at the moment, from family to government.

What I am hinting at here is a kind of emotional male left-wingism, in which the man can liberate himself from role, from life as cog and gear, from stereotype, and graduate into a position from which he can see himself and his mother as living, breathing people, passionate, heated, meaningful—and that mother is not a huge breast that extends through the walls of the nursery out into the world and that must always be pumped for satisfaction.

The good mother is a *woman*. And being a woman, she is human. Anything less and she is a caricature who breeds caricatures.

Let's get a bit deeper into this idea.

The mother we have been describing, an unsafe, self-revealing woman, with her stimulation of pleasure and pain, her inner wildness and desire to rebel and break loose from social bonds, can communicate to her son one of the greatest gifts a mother can pass on: imagination. Nothing independent, hence nothing individual or different, can be accomplished without imagination. Without imagination the son will play out his roles in life for better or worse, usually for worse because a man who assumes roles joins a system, an ism, and thereby loses his identity, while illusorily believing that he has an identity—which he does only insofar as some group defines it. He is allowed to *think* that he has an identity, but should he go his own way, seek his personal identity, he will probably be ostracized from the group and treated as if he were *nothing*. In this sense the groups in the larger world are parallels to the family group, which is run by the need to conform. This no doubt is a vestige from primitive times, when families needed to stay bound together for their very survival. But many families still believe that they must work under the survival ethic—except that the ethic is more and more being broadened to include society, country, whatever. Thus there is no surprise in the fact that whenever things begin to fall apart in society—as has been dramatically happening in the United States for the last two decades—sociologists and psychiatrists immediately publish articles linking the collapse of society to the collapse of the nuclear family.

What this means, in essence, is that when family controls and structure fail to parallel those of society, there is no feed-in machine to spew out cogs for the larger social power plant. The family, then, is not doing its part to keep society stable. But the thought that this breakdown might be a dissolution from which something new emerges is rarely thought of, rarely considered. People are too busy panicking.

Now it is precisely the "good mother" who contributes significantly to this dissolution. She does not preach rebellion or anarchy on a soapbox; she does not tell everybody in the family that the revolution has come. What she does is to take her repressive and stifling tradition of compliance, submission, and unconsciously throw it to the winds. For the American and European woman, it has been her sacred duty to produce worthwhile male members to keep society not balanced but stable—stable and hence stagnant. Given a period of time with this stagnation and we have the phenomenon of senators and congressmen urging a President to rattle some sabers internationally—in essence, just for the hell of it.

But when a mother begins to subvert the sacred family group by communicating to her son (which she will do more powerfully, even though subtly, than to her daughter, because most women still have the feeling that rebellion is masculine) that something is wrong, that many more things are possible, that life really has no rules—in short, when she subliminally conveys to her son that rebellion is possible, yet gives him enough opposition so that he can *effect* the rebellion—then the rebellion takes place through an act of intense and vibrant imagination.

In other words, she makes it possible for her son to break their symbiotic bond, permitting him to become his own man in the only way that a man can—through a rebellion and moving away from dependency and familial stagnation and control.

Note that I said she *permits* him. He does it by himself, but she has laid the groundwork for the possibility. You can be free, she lets him know. Take your freedom. Yet most of the time she does not even know she is doing this, and will react badly when her son begins to take the freedom she has subtly, unknowingly, allowed him to take.

So that the good mother, as I am describing her in this way, is a mother who can also be depriving. Depriving to the point of not allowing her son to become swallowed by her ever-flowing breast. And she is dominating too, dominating enough to give her son something against which to rebel, to break free of—but not dominating to the point of robbing his soul and perhaps sending him to the madhouse. She gives him always a bit less than he needs, she makes him reach, so that he can see that there are possibilities in the world greater than she can offer him.

This may *seem* like a double message: the conscious, waking-life message is given that the son should be a good boy, love his mother, listen to her and obey her rules—while her inner life is subtly propelling him, and at times not so subtly propelling him, toward rebellion, freedom. But it isn't really a double message at all, not if the underlying message is listened to—as it always is. The conflict is necessary; it is the only thing that propels one toward growth—and in the conflict is *enormous* pain. But without the pain there is no differentiation, no separation from the mother, and one becomes a frightened, dependent social vegetable.

Such a mother does *not* want to destroy her son. The inconsistency of the message shows this. She is merely giving him something to overcome, to fight against; for if she were to remove the obstacle, the fight would be over and there would be no freedom ever. Because every time she gives her son opposition and resistance, the underside of the coin appears—the side of rebellion and manhood. Her behavior immediately calls up its opposite because she has laid the groundwork for precisely that response. Her posture of dominance immediately triggers off the necessity of revolt; her criticism can immediately let her son focus on his own strengths; and her attacks can also stimulate a knowledge of his own strengths.

It is all in the doing, in the *being*. The son will for years remain in a state of anger at his mother because of her lack of acceptance and approval—and that anger is the key to whatever liberation will be achieved. The context of anger keeps the separation from mother going on, until one day the relationship with his mother will be seen more clearly for what it is.

The anger we are dealing with here is solely the anger that results in the boy as a reaction to feelings of domination and control, of the frustration of *his* needs—an anger that, if properly channeled, becomes tempered into the valuable tool of assertiveness. *Self-assertion.* A sense of his life as *his* life, to do with as *he* sees fit.

A mother who cannot stimulate anger in her son cannot be a good mother, cannot even be a true person. She is a saint, and her son will be paralyzed with guilt whenever he has a wish to smite the saint. But the mother who acts in such a way that anger is a necessity—that is a mother who knows something about the necessity to be independent.

Freedom is contingent. There is no such thing as absolute freedom, for what has bound us to our mothers in the early moments of our lives can never be washed away. And so men frequently take early steps toward freedom by doing everything they can to be different from their mothers—to become liberal if she is conservative, tolerant if she is intolerant, atheistic if she is religious.

And while this can lead to hellish confrontations, wrenching emotional scenes, alienations—a picture of complete disharmony—that is only what happens on the surface. Within, all is consistent: the son is unerringly obeying his mother's unconscious edict to take his liberty and get the hell out of the nest.

The conflict here can of course last through life, with no seeing into it, without seeing into the hidden inner message.

That is too bad, but that's the way it might have to be—until such time as we all can admit what we are really doing without the necessity for pretense, without a mother's necessity to take her own freedom, while remaining locked into the maternal role, by pushing her son out to become independent *for* her; and until such time that a man cannot think that his independence has *nothing* to do with his mother's permission.

Even when the son can make some peace with all of this, he might simply have to keep it to himself although he may want to share it with his mother. A man says:

> After so many years of fights and struggles and pure misery I'm grateful to her. All I ever wanted from her was acceptance, but she would never give me that.
> I spent years blaming and accusing her for undermining me, for making me neurotic and sick, for screwing up my life. And when I finally came to understand and accept what she had really given me—a sense of flair, an emotionalism, a way of not accepting everything at face value, the ability to suffer pain in order to find out who I really was, to find out that Jews were okay, that orthodox religion was not for me—I mean in general the need to be different from others, well, there was just no way to share that with her because she must still behave as if she stands against all of that.
>
> How do you say, "Thank you for giving me the stuff to be different from you. Thank you for giving me the courage to fight you, to fight against the woman who gave birth to me. Thank you for having enough inside of you to give that to me even though you couldn't do it yourself."
>
> How do you say that? Well, I don't think you can.

You can't bring that home to her. Some place inside, she would know it's true, but she couldn't say so, couldn't let herself see that.

Because, you know, one thing has come clear to me: she gave me the possibility to be free enough from her because she gave me the courage to be enraged at her. But how, if she ever agreed with me now, could she be free herself without her own anger? She needs to be angry at me for her own independence the same as I needed to be angry at her for mine.

How I'd love to share that with her! And how useless it would be to try.

So the good mother seems to conform to her role, to the eternal verities, as if following some predetermined pattern to maintain stability. But within she is wild, a rebel, and in the little understood playing-out of the maternal ritual, she is somehow helping to liberate her son.

And this is the thrust into life.

FIVE

OUTSIDE, LOOKING IN: THE FATHER

By the time a father can relate to his son on a verbal level—talk to him, be with him in any other than a chin-chucking way—he is an outsider. True, a father may hold his infant son, feed him bottles, involve himself in a number of infant-raising exercises—but he is a peripheral figure, he is not a person of crucial and dynamic impact in forming the world-view of his son. He is more or less a shadowy figure in his son's world, whether he is always present or not present at all. The father may be there, but he is a person whose very existence has been interpreted by the mother, whose very presence is permitted by the mother—and later a man whose actions, whose absences, whose proclivities, habits, and ways of being in his own world, will be interpreted by the mother to her son.

This state of affairs exists in every culture, East and

West, and even in some cultures we still call "primitive." (I remember with amusement an Indian film fresh from Bombay entitled *I Kill for Mother*—with especial amusement because of the myth, lately put to rest by Indira Ghandhi, that Indian women are thoroughly servile.) Even in the United States, where men are appearing to become more involved in child rearing, fathers are much more comfortable relating to their sons when a more verbal, more "logical" level of communication is reached.

Certainly a great deal of communicating, of training, of "being with" can take place on this level, but it will rest on the foundation already laid by the mother–son relationship. It is no accident that Freud and a host of his followers stressed intellectual knowledge, verbal communication (the "talking cure"), and cognitive, rational insight. It is a masculine psychology which places little emphasis on nonverbal insight, and Freud's early women followers fell into his masculine camp.

Men talk, men are rational—and it is along these lines that fathers are more at home dealing with their sons. They can have a potent impact upon their sons as individuals *separate* from the maternal world, but this requires great effort and patience, and a gift for delicate arbitration. In short, it's a full-time job—and men simply do not seem to have the inclination for it or the time to engage in it. And so the mother's world remains paramount, and the father is only a figure in it—at times as he is, at times as an invention, almost a fictional character.

What emerges here is a task for the father: Who am I in my son's world? And how do I go about establishing *my own identity* in the eyes of my son? The task is formidable, and only slightly less so even when a father gains some understanding of the primal bond between mother and son.

It all begins very early, and it begins without any conscious hostility or competition on the mother's part. Listen to a sensitive man describing it:

It was a Friday and I'd been able to leave work early. When I got home Jane was feeding the baby and I watched as I used to like to do. I wished I could be that close to him. He turned his head away from her breast for a moment and looked at me briefly—and I thought of our cat. Cats sort of check your presence sometimes, but there doesn't seem to be any comment involved in it. When he went back to Jane's breast I rubbed my knuckle softly against his cheek, and again I was reminded of the cat: while a cat eats you can fluff its head or tickle its ears and it goes right on eating. You're sort of not there.

I watched their involvement together and I felt, not shut out exactly, but not a *part* of it. I would never be a part of that kind of intimacy—and I wondered, good Lord, is the first time I'll have an impact on the kid when I toss a baseball around with him? I knew that wasn't so, that there would be contact of all sorts, but it seemed so long to wait—so very long. I wondered what he would begin to recognize me as.

This would seem a conscientious man, perhaps overly so—but yet perhaps not. He began to reflect on his relationship with his wife, began to prowl about in the corners of her world, began to wonder what he would find in his son when the child was old enough to see him outside the physical and emotional world of his wife.

Loving his wife, enjoying their relationship, he could find himself confident. Their worlds seemed largely compatible. He felt secure that his wife would not distort him, felt secure that their two worlds overlapped to an extent that would allow his son to form a bond with him later. In essence, he felt secure that he was not an alien in the world of his wife and that she would not cause his son to become a stranger to him—strangers to each other.

But he can't really *know* this. He can only trust that it's so, that his reasoning and faith are by and large accurate. He can only hope. But the one thing that he can know, does know, is that "I can never become part of the bond *they* have together. God, it's almost occult—I mean what they have together. Sometimes he looks at me, not like the cat, but like a little boy, and he seems to know something about me. But what? What can he know? But he knows something—and *I* haven't been his teacher."

Even with his faith he can have this fantasy:

I will come home from work one day and suddenly he will be standing there in short pants and shoes and all the rest of it, stick out his hand, and say, "Hello." And I'll shake it and say, "Let me introduce myself: I'm your father." And he'll say, "Yes, I know," and tell me all of what he knows about me and I won't have the faintest idea who he's talking about.

This, as I've said, is a sensitive man—sensitive because he can feel these things, make these observations about the relationship between his wife and son.

But more often than not, in fact the rule and hardly the exception, is that none of this is seen at all—and the fantasy becomes reality: the mother–son bond, because of its intensity and symbiosis, is so established around the mother's world-view that indeed son and father stand as strangers to each other.

Later they play together, mother and son, and the world

of play becomes another way in which the boy is instructed, shaped, urged on into life and mastery—or narrowed, controlled, his natural resources weakened.

I watch my four-year-old playing with my mother. They are ostensibly cooperating in building something from Lincoln Logs. My boy is getting desultory, removed, a bit sulky—and he never sulks, or rarely. He says what he means or he doesn't say what he means. He almost never sulks. I watch. I see that every time he places a log where he wants it, where he wants it to be in the house *he* wishes to build [and later as a man he will want to build some sort of edifice for himself, he will want to construct the edifice of *his* life], I see that every time he wants to exercise *his* creativity, his will, my mother wants it differently. He wants a large window in the log cabin, she wants a smaller one; he wants a roof of five green slats, she wants one of four; he tries to create a large door, for her the need is for a smaller one.

Finally he has had enough. After a moment of immobilization in his final sulk, he tosses the logs from his hand, says "Forget it," and walks off. And I say to myself, "You're a better man than I."

That may be true. He may become a better man than I. I hope he will.

But the point is: *my* mother is not *his* mother. He can go home at the end of the day; he can break up the game. And it surely seems as if he doesn't give a damn about what she thinks.

But I could not have left.

I could not have thrown down my little batch of logs.

My house would finally not have been mine.
My house would have been hers.

The larger issue for the future of the boy who lives through the myriad experiences of contact with his mother is how his world becomes sculpted for him—and one can see it in this kind of play. But even on a concrete level, a completely nonsymbolic level, how many times has an incident like the log-cabin encounter resulted in the adult man allowing his wife not only to construct a world for him but to literally choose the house in which he will live? And how many times can the malaise of the middle-class man, the man to whom "something happened" as Joseph Heller would state it, be directly pinned to, be deeply rooted in, the incredible passivity with which he has allowed his wife (whose intentions may be the purest) to recapitulate the world of his childhood—recapituating it without toys, but in adult dress and trappings?

But again, we must look at this situation, this private world of the mother–son bond, keeping our observations as free of value judgment as possible. Mothers have been blamed for far too many mishaps, as if they had no internal pressures, no warps, no troubles—as if they were able to stand above it all, having purged themselves of all needs for power, control, and love. Perhaps, on a level beyond conscious awareness, people do not want to see them as human beings—again, ambivalent human beings—engaged in a human activity, as human beings who seek something in their relationships with their sons.

Mothers make fine scapegoats.

They make fine scapegoats because their role has been mythologized, their function raised to the level of the sacred, and in the Catholic faith their heroine and model is the mother of Christ. Odd that the washing of soiled diapers, the constant cleaning, feeding, waking half drugged with weariness in the middle of the night, the self-tortures of guilt—odd that all of these very human, utterly mundane events should be raised to sainthood.

How easy it is, then, to feel disappointed when she lets us down. How easy to attack an abstraction, an impossible ideal. How almost impossibly difficult for men to relate to her as a *person*.

The Virgin Mary. The Mother of Christ. No matter what one's religion or lack of it, Mary has a pointed and very powerful meaning for us. Through prayers, through supplications to her, she will intercede. She will carry our pleas to her son who is God and hence his own father—and he will never refuse her. He will comply with her wish, will grant the desire in the prayer. For she is the perfect screening device; she will never bring to him something trivial. She may have to exert great pressure on him in a cause she espouses—but she will bring to him only that which she knows he will honor. He accepts her world and will do what she asks.

On our human level the parallel is striking, the parallel to the mother–son bond. For it is a tight world, outside of which the father stands, trying to peer in. No matter how "good" or solid a woman's experience has been with her father, then later with her husband, she is the root of the relationship with her son, while the father is initially a sort of constant visitor, part of the household. In the worst of cases he is like the family dog, friendly and snappish by turns; in the best of cases he is involved. But it is there in that primal mother–son interaction that the son's world begins to be formed, filtered through the vision of the mother, with all its realities and distortions.

My five-year-old son is flying to the West Coast with his mother and sister and will be gone for two weeks. He knows me, he may or may not have accepted my absences from him, and I know he misses me and I miss him when we are away from each other.

On the eve of the flight he looks at me, cocks his head, grins, and says, "I'm going on an airplane tomorrow and I'll never see Daddy again." And then waits.

I reassure him and he says he will phone me, and even though everybody has my number he copies it down fresh, for himself. The number is *our* bond, established in *that* moment, but I know that he won't use it. But that isn't the point. He is making a contact, a contact of the mind, a kind of mini–business deal—and I suspect that we, son and father, will always have to make that kind of bond to touch base. It is a piece of magic, that number; as long as he has it, it will be a connecting link across two thousand miles.

I may live inside him, he may have images of me, but I do not, cannot ever, live inside him with the force and omnipresence of his mother. They *have* each other.

Fathers can and do have impact—when they can get through the crack in the door. But the less they try, the more they feel shut out; the less they *see* in the bond between mother and son, the more shadowy they become, the more they edge out toward the periphery, away from the world of that bond, a spacewalk into the mist of conjecture and ambiguity.

My small son is playing with a Sesame Street "dollhouse": two tenements peopled by little wooden figures of all the characters who daily badger him from out of the colored tube. There is Big Bird and Bert and Ernie and Mr. Hooper and all the rest, with tiny TV sets, tables, chairs, beds, and Oscar the Grouch yakking out of his garbage can.

My son is doing something very different today, and for some minutes I watch him silently with my natural observational streak that helps make me a therapist and a writer. He amasses in front of the twin tenements a fleet of trucks, fire engines, and an ambulance—and then begins to move everything. All the people, all the furniture, stacking them in the backs of the trucks, and I am somehow reminded of the Okies in *The Grapes of Wrath*, so intense is he in what he is doing, so serious. And then I remember that a nuclear reactor in Pennsylvania has gone blooey, people are being evacuated, and there has been much talk in the house of fleeing if weather conditions drive the radiation closer.

The world has suddenly become dangerous for him—mysteriously dangerous since he knows nothing of nuclear radiation. I have sensed a kind of hysteria around the issue, and it has gotten to him. And as he drives the host of cars and trucks away I wonder where he will go with them. I wonder how he will cope with this.

And I am pleased, happy. He gets his procession to the end of the room, turns everything around, and begins to drive back to the tenements. "They're moving into a new place now," he says, and begins unloading, placing the little people and the furniture in the rooms. I am happy he can see security somewhere else—that if he has to flee, he can go somewhere, go *to* somewhere and not just run.

But what he has reacted to is *fear*, anxiety—not the fear of what he can see, know, understand, and *then* fear, but of a world suddenly turned dangerous because he has been told it is dangerous. And he really doesn't know, can't know, why.

Now, having waited and watched it all, I must see if I can do anything about it. I must see if I can help balance his vision and defuse some of the anxiety.

We can see that the boy has a good sense of security, that he knows he can find someplace to go. But something has been planted within him that may or may not fester, that may be completely resolved because it will have no meaning past the moment, the specific time in which it took place. But something might linger on—the beginning of a sense, a belief, that his world can become incomprehensibly threatening, by things he can't see, can't cope with. If this does indeed develop, he may be slightly anxious whenever he wishes to do something new and daring. Later in life he may recall the whole event quite clearly—the facts of it. But it will do no good. The facts will be split from the perception. Threat was introduced into his world. And so it will be.

The boy automatically trusts that his mother can interpret the world for him. There is no thought process in this. It emanates from the closeness of the bond. The father can step in when he sees some gross distortion taking shape in the boy's world, but his intervention very often leads only to a kind of trembling confusion on the part of the child. This confusion, a natural reaction when confronted with contradictory messages, becomes unbearable should the mother *need* to communicate a world-view entirely different from her husband's in order to "stay on top" or shut him out.

As it is, if the boy's mother said something, it is correct, it must be correct; pull a piece out and the whole structure wobbles, the whole world may come suddenly apart. The child can't take the contradiction, the ambiguity. Which is why, when a father steps in and says to his son, "No, there's no real danger, everything will be all right," the boy will say, "Uh-uh," usually shaking his head. "Uh-uh. Mommy said."

This is why it is so unbearably difficult, or at least such a delicate proposition, for a father to enter the mother–son world. The boy's world has been continually shaped, structured, formed—but not in analytic pieces and parts, distinct and separate entities, not in any way along the lines of adult reasoning or logic. That world they share is a global world, all of a piece, seamless, and he has to keep it that way or suffer intense anxiety and fear. It will be emotional light-years before he can say, "My mother is wrong about that." He cannot do it while his world is still in the process of formation. So he must reject any outside intervention— and the father is an outsider.

Most child psychologists are staunch advocates of a united front on the part of parents when discipline is required. Quite simply, mother and father should agree on discipline so as not to confuse the child. But it takes no professional to see that what this ends up as in most respects is the father's agreement with the disciplinary line proposed by the mother. It *is* united on the surface, but what has happened is that the father has been pulled into the mother's system and he ends up merely acquiescing, not really sharing in the process. So the child sees that they are united, but he doesn't see his father as an individual in any way. He simply sees his mother's system being once more acted upon. He has no ally. He belongs to his mother, and so does his father—and his perception of her as the ultimate power, the goddess of his world, is reaffirmed.

He still doesn't see who his father is—and from there will begin to emanate the complaint so common in later life: my father did everything my mother wanted; she ran him; he didn't care. And all the rest.

It takes a very long time, and much self-probing, much inner awareness, before a man can look back at his childhood and realize that what he is complaining about is an *adult* view of his father's so-called indifference, an adult view with adult thought processes and adult value judgments, all linked to anger and perhaps a measure of bitterness at what he felt deprived of. It takes a long time for him to realize that his mother was the shaper of his world, and that not only did his father not disrupt it, but that *he himself* could not have permitted such a disruption, such an intrusion.

This can be a stunning revelation, but a revelation that most men rarely come to, because unless they have been deeply hurt in very direct ways by their mothers, the possibility is never explored. And for a very simple reason: it is difficult, if not almost impossible, to see why you are unhappy in your world, unhappy with your mother, if you are still living in that world. Conversely, if you *are* happy, what is there to question?

Where the revelation often takes place is in psychotherapy—the seeking of which presupposes at least some degree of discontent—where the current world as one sees it may be gradually taken apart and examined. And with men, a remarkable thing takes place—the rule and not the exception. The anger first emerges, usually, at the father—who wasn't present, who let one down, who thought he was being a good father because he tossed around a football. Ultimately, he was a bust, a flop, he probably ran around with other women, he hurt his wife. Mother was fine, she put up with a lot—at times she was a saint.

And then, after a litany of complaints and anger, the well suddenly runs dry and the man feels stuck. There seems no further place to go. And all a therapist has to do is say, "Mother was a saint," and then comes a torrent of rage that can wilt flowers. It can go on and on in almost hysterical paroxysms; it seems as if it will never end. But it does end, and a process of separation begins—the identifying of the components of the world they created together, the weeding out of the destructive elements from the positive elements—a process which must be accomplished if life is to have any balance.

For in that bonded world of mother and son are elements of what worked to keep the son infantile and dependent as well as what urged him into life, into, as we have come to say, "the good things." And only when this duality is understood, and its components recognized, can that primal internal relationship be seen for what it was.

All men are familiar with a general complaint: "Nothing I can do will ever please my mother. I've tried and tried, and she just won't accept me." And all men are familiar with the repeated efforts of knocking on that sealed door, the scraped, bleeding psychic knuckles, the lack of response, the perpetual criticism, the lament of rage and frustration: My God, what does she *want?* What does she want that I can never give her, why does she turn me back? It makes many men feel totally condemned and at times totally worthless, failures. Men can look at their lives and think they are fine, productive—but when she looks down her nose at them they even begin to question what they thought they were sure of only five minutes before.

But recall the man whose mother refused to allow him to take the pledge in church. He sees something between the lines, sees something emerging into the light. He sees that in some way he has become what he is happy to be because his mother encouraged him, urged him, in the direction he took—and it no longer matters to him that his mother urged him in his new direction by setting herself up as an ultimate power. On some level he rather likes it. He admires her for it. Because he finds meaning now in what he is.

And he understands that she wished him to be (covertly, except for her few isolated public displays of defiance) exactly what she wished to be herself, but could not muster the *courage* to be.

He became the man she always wanted for herself. He became the ideal man—the man she would have married if she could have, the man she wished to bring into the world. Ultimately, the kind of human being *she* wished to be. But to confront this would be too frightening to her and so she must continue to oppose him, not accept him.

They are both very powerful people. *He* is the man. His father collects coins, does crossword puzzles, watches the eleven o'clock news and professes puzzlement about the state of the world, and tells him to be good to his mother.

While the father is out of it in this relationship, as he seems to be in so many of the encounters between mothers and sons—where the mother–son bond is so intense that he *must* stay out of it or lose face by being *chased* out of it—there is another sort of relationship which, if the top layers are peeled away, becomes quite obvious. This is where the

boy perceives his father as the power, the chief, the dominant member of the household, and being frightened of
him, moves closer and closer to his mother, whom he sees
as kind, soft, all-giving—and ultimately a victim.

But inside this familiar triangle, very often it is the
mother who has constructed the myth of the father's control—which is a sort of opposite effect to the father telling
his son to "do it for your mother." Here she cultivates an
image of her husband's domination and power so as to stand
free of, away from, her son's anger and bad feelings: they in
essence form a united front against the "tyrannical" father.

"I wish you wouldn't do this because you know how
your father will take it."

"Please don't say anything about this. You know how
your father flies into a rage."

"I don't suppose it will do any good, but you should ask
your father anyway."

Ad infinitum.

She and he remain bonded, united, conspiratorial—and
the boy will forever feel more comfortable in the presence
of women, anxious and frightened in the presence of men.

And it is all an illusion.

In most cases, the mother is not contriving this power
shift in any kind of consciously manipulative way; she simply has profound difficulties in handling a man, any man
(perhaps even any woman) who has his own wishes, own
desires for independence, and hence his own angers and
rebellions. And she certainly doesn't want these things from
her son, so she forms a bond of strength with the boy
against her husband—who is cast in the role of villain. And
the good prince defends her against the bad king who, like
Henry VIII, can consign her to a dungeon or lop off her
head.

It is a fairy tale acted out—like so many of the fairy tales acted out in all our relationships—as Joseph Campbell pointed out in his *Hero with a Thousand Faces*, in which a man crossing the street in the middle of New York City is living in a nursery fairy tale of loving mother and fearing father. Living in it, immersed in it, having it activate and dampen a huge portion of his life—while crossing the street on his way to work in the "larger" world.

But what of the father in this particular fairy story? Why, if he is not truly a villain—and obviously a host of fathers and husbands *are*—why, if he is not really a heavy, a hissed-at, black-bearded, turn-of-the-century stage villain, does he accept the role forged from his wife's script? He says nothing to contradict this situation because he does not know how to pick up the reins of true responsibility and authority. He lets this false image be foisted on him, even though its repercussions are powerful, its distortions obvious, and its ramifications often heartbreaking, because it is the only way he knows how to appear powerful, in command. In essence, his wife is his mommy, and his mommy is giving him permission to be a "big man." As long as he doesn't interfere.

And in fact the situation frequently escalates. Given the permission to be the "big man," he may not simply sit back and silently enjoy his "powerful" position while his wife and son do their own thing (alas, the fabled absent father); he may rise to the occasion and actively compete with his son. His son then in a way becomes a sibling, while they share the same mother. And it isn't always obvious:

I was always afraid of him. Why, I never knew. He stayed aloof, removed, almost withdrawn. He didn't seem to be around, if you know what I mean. And it all began to torture me when I failed out of prep school. All the instructors were male and I was terrified of *them*. I saw a shrink years later and I got into Freud a little, but my father was *not* blatantly authoritarian, and I was confused and feeling very creepy and lost and really very hopeless—like the whole men-fear thing was genetic and absolutely irreversible. I even wondered if I was some sort of constitutional homosexual—which at that point would have been fine with me if I had the balls even to approach a man on any kind of level. Total incompetence; I couldn't compete with a male oyster.

Then one day I was watching my four-year-old nephew hammering nails into an old carving board. Just hammering them in for the hell of it—and I almost bolted out of my chair. There it was—there it was for *me*, at least. A flood of memories came back to me—not new ones, but memories I never paid much attention to. My father would never let *me* hammer anything without taking the thing away and showing me how to do it—and finally doing it himself. He wouldn't let me set up my Christmas trains. He even threw a ball to me so low or so wide that I couldn't catch it.

And he would just shake his head. My mother would always give me milk and cookies and put her arm around my shoulder. But he just shook his head.

Outside, looking in. Powerful, resentful, competitive. Looking in at the bond, unable to take part in any meaningful way except through silent intimidation.

On the other hand, there is a different kind of chaos

that can result when a father, if he finally does, attempts to take control.

It happens when he tries to break the bond—or if not break it, then simply to dent it, bend it. He attempts to have some say in the way his son is being brought up—and is promptly rebuffed:

Father says, "We can let him stay up a little longer tonight. He's getting into basketball now and wants to watch the playoff game."

"No," says mother. "It will just make him crabby in the morning and tired all day."

"Well, why not just this once?"

"Look, *you* don't have to live with him all day. I do."

The father is stung by her refusal. True, he doesn't have to live with his son during the day, but he wants to live with him *now*, sharing some situation or event when they can. But he has to bow out: their sharing will cause some kind of terrible inconvenience for his wife. He begins to feel accused that he works during the day—and yet work he must. What is it, then, that he is really being accused of? Lack of consideration? Of sensitivity?

He can push on, plug away, but there never seems to be a way in. And then it dawns on him; he finally gets it. He can share time with his son when, only when, his wife permits him to—and then he becomes resentful, angry. And ultimately may face what drives most fathers into paroxysms of rage:

"What do you say we watch the basketball game tonight?"

"Mommy doesn't like it when I stay up too late."

That is usually the crusher, the clincher. He accuses his wife of controlling his son, or of trying to keep them apart. And he may begin to develop a deep angry contempt for his son—a contempt very often compounded by self-contempt. Because neither of them—the man nor the boy—can buck the system. So he watches the game with a six-pack of beer, muttering under his breath, feeling shut away from both wife and son.

In days gone by, things were different—the father actively trying to introduce his son into an adult male world, the much-written-about, nostalgia-ridden tales of fathers who took their sons to burlesque shows or later in life to fancy brothels, trained them to follow in their footsteps in their businesses or trades, taught them how to tend the fields and do the chores.

But that is largely over now, and what we are left with is the myth of *being with*—of tossing a football around on a Sunday, of scoutmastering . . . the myth of family togetherness, the forcing of a triangle between mother, father, and son into some "wholesome" pattern of sunny faces at the breakfast table, fun-filled picnics, joint decisions (in which some adult always wins anyway), etc., etc.

And there is little truth in any of it. Because it is all so obviously forced, as believable as a four-color ad in a Sunday supplement.

The family that stays together . . .

A pause here lest we conclude that a father is ultimately a futile appendage, and nothing more, to the mother–son relationship. Or worse, that he can only damage his son.

My observation over many years is that men rarely question the motives of fatherhood—although they often express vociferous regrets when facing the pressures of bringing up children. And the majority of women don't question their desire to become mothers. Aside from biological drives or wishes to create life or to produce something from love and sharing—processes that men seem in awe of and largely out of touch with—women's growing awareness often reveals wishes to compete with friends who have children, to satisfy the perceived "commands" of their parents, to have the "experience" purely because they *can* have it, to avoid engagement with other aspects of living, ad infinitum. (Influential European feminists are beginning to define the sacrosanct "maternal instinct" as a myth.)

But modern men never seem to have reasons; or if they do, their reasons apparently defy articulation. And not knowing, not being in touch, a man somehow by default slides into one of our great social clichés: the Role Model. The cornerstone of the role model is *masculinity*: a man must be fully heterosexual, rational, success oriented, competitive—and this example is supposed to be communicated to the son. Be like me. Do what I do. The emptiness of this position reverberates hollowly.

Why be a father? To satisfy a wife? To keep her housebound? To demonstrate virility? To have a possession? To play catch?

For men it is no longer a self-defined process: today no one is keeping the hardware business in the family, no one needs cheap family labor on the truck farm. Boys can no longer describe accurately what their fathers *do* all day. "My father is a psychologist and talks to people." "My father has ideas to sell products." "My father wears a suit and tie and goes to work someplace in the city."

So what a father must do in these days of corporate and

industrial anonymity is become aware of the *internal* process propelling him to fatherhood—and this is a task of the profoundest self-exploration. What is my responsibility to my son—to my son who *did not request his birth*—and how can I fulfill that responsibility in cooperation and accord with his mother?

The paternal role requires a complete overhauling and a wholesale redefinition. So does the entire concept of parenthood.

This overhauling and self-exploration require courage and effort; the stereotyped role model is too easily adopted, too passive, too reliant on irrelevant tradition. Men must themselves grow up and find true meaning and value in their own lives before they can wield a full positive effect on their sons. Otherwise they remain the "absent father" and passively shunt off parental responsibility to the mother.

Still today, in the context of traditional psychotherapy, the role model is adhered to overtly or tacitly. Father is companion, arbiter, superego, never nurturer or explorer. He is to maintain societal values, however rusty and creaky, and show his son the way. And this position often leads to the unrealistic question asked of a male patient who complains of maternal domination: "Didn't your father ever step in between you and your mother?"

What we usually see is the chaos that results when a father attempts to penetrate his son's bond with his mother. Such attempts ultimately result in the accusation that he is trying to destroy or undermine family "unity," that he is "confusing" his son by running counter to the day-by-day discipline of the household. But what he is really doing when he steps in is rebelling against his wife—and perhaps even more deeply, rebelling against the mother in his wife who is calling the tune for the household, for his son, as his own mother called the tune for *him*.

To want to see his son set free is to want to see himself set free.

But more often than not, he will lose this battle too. Because he will be faced with the same hostility and accusations—and threatened loss of love—that he was afraid of when he was a boy himself.

And, quite simply, most men just give up. It isn't worth it.

A man may end up staying out of it entirely, and by so doing, will lose the last shreds of his identity—or, better put, the last shreds of individuality *as seen by his son*.

He comes home less frequently. He works longer hours. Suddenly more chores need to be done on weekends. And eventually, when he walks into the house, he is indeed a stranger and his son begins to see him as an alien who carries about him some aura of contempt, anger, fear, disgust, and a kind of irritable depression—a sardonic, cutting tone, a mordant wit, sullen impatience.

On the eve of a marital breakup a woman says:

> Tommy and I were doing a jigsaw puzzle when my husband came home late from work. He had a kind of leer on his face—well, not a leer, but his lip was curled and he was definitely mad about something, and looked sort of ferocious. I put my arm around Tommy's shoulder, I guess I was scared or something. And I guess that did it. He growled and Tommy began to cry and clutch on to me, and he said, "That's better—and I might as well really give you something to be scared of." He kicked the jigsaw pieces all over the room and walked out. Tommy cried for almost an

hour. I knew my husband had a mean streak and I always tried to protect Tommy from it—but that night we really saw it, and I couldn't protect him from it any longer.

"I knew my husband had a mean streak and *I always tried to protect Tommy from it* ..."

For some reason tied to his own problems, her husband felt so brutally shut out of that relationship that there was no way on earth he could participate in it—let alone step in between his wife and son. And so he opted out. And what of his "mean streak"? Was it always there? Was it always there and finally erupted? Or was it simply his frustrated response because the mother's arm would encircle his son's shoulder whenever he entered a room, or raised his voice, or mumbled?

Who can tell?

But someday, when asked what kind of man his father was, the grown-up son might simply say, "My father? He was a mean bastard."

And yet it can be different—an impressionistic picture of an opposite sort, vastly different in content. A man tells us:

I never saw my father. He joined the navy during the Second World War while my mother was pregnant. He was assigned to a destroyer and was killed in the Battle of Midway. I suppose I got a lot of sympathy from people and for a time my friends sort of regarded me as a kind of hero once removed—at least up until the time that memories of that war faded and no one cared anymore. But I grew up very proud of my father, I felt I had some kind of glorious lineage—a lineage of warriors and heroes. And I knew that my

sense of his strength and greatness was hammered
home because my mother never remarried, never even
went out with a man as far as I know. Because, you
see, no one could ever match up to my hero father.

One of my aunts is a tippler and she gets very
loose when she's had a few. She and my mother have
always had some kind of bitter rivalry which ends up
by one or the other of them telling gossipy, vicious
stories about the other when they're on the outs.

So Aunt Mary had a few belts one night, was on
the outs with my mother again, and told me the
whole story. Well, actually there wasn't much to tell,
except that my father took off when I was about six
months old and never came back. Somebody saw him
once after that pumping gas on Route 4 in New
Jersey—or at least they thought they saw him. And
that was it. He never sent my mother a penny for me
or for herself. That was *it*.

I didn't know what to do. I was enraged and I felt
sort of crazy, as if I didn't know who part of myself
was. I had been a Boy Scout, in ROTC in college
and a lieutenant in the army—was it possible that all
that came from the myth of my hero father? All that
masculinity? You could swear that I had some big
strong father to model myself after all my life.

It hit me that my mother was my mother *and* my
father, and I can't tell you how crazy *that* made me
feel.

We had a brutal, almost unbearable scene when
I confronted her with it, but she finally admitted it.
She said, "All I wanted to do was give you a good
father to remember, not some bum who deserted us."

I could understand that, but the whole thing is

too complicated to go into—and besides, what for? What would I be trying to be find out by slicing it into bits and pieces? But I still feel creepy about it.

And with all this, the question must again arise: Is everything distorted? Isn't there any situation which isn't filled with fantasies, wish-fulfillments, lies, the satisfaction of only personal needs, and all the rest? Of course, but never free of personal needs—although the satisfaction of them doesn't have to be twisted or fabricated.

There are mothers who can keep these things to a minimum, who can be in touch, who don't necessarily have to turn their sons into some fantasied versions of the men they wish they had married—or the men they long for, men who will come and rescue them from their prisons or long sleeps.

There are some solid relationships in which parenting is shared, contradiction and opposing views are tolerated, and many problems about child raising are worked out—where both parents appreciate their sense of independence without being overly threatened by rejection or abandonment. There are even separated parents who do not engage in the bitterness toward each other that takes the form of bad-mouthing each other to their children.

And as there are men who genuinely like women, like them and respect them as women and people, so too are there women who feel positively about men—who do not seek to make men over in some needed image and so do not choose men who want some woman to do this.

And these are the women, the mothers, who can as far as possible allow their boys to be boys, then men, but who at the same time can contribute to their male children a sense of possessing qualities of "womanness," a receptivity, a creativity, an intuition that allows the male child to possess the best aspects of what we can only call androgyny —or what Jung would call being in touch with the *anima*, the female principle, the depths of the soul. And how? Simply by allowing the boy to know, feel, sense that he has two parents, one male, the other female, and instead of making him over into some fantasied image of what a man should be, allowing him to develop into a person in touch with maleness and femaleness instead of a parody—a brittle, reactive human being who equates all softness with weakness, vulnerability and, ultimately, homosexuality.

If women, mothers, will understand themselves, will become in touch with their inner power, a power that is unique to them, then they will not need to see men as powerful—but just as men.

And when it happens, as it surely one day must, good Lord, what a mothering experience we will see.

And what men, what *real men*, will be born upon this earth.

My plane was late but I arrived just in time for my uncle's funeral. My father's brother. He was a good mechanic, a filling-station owner whose heart had given out after two earlier attacks. A simple, direct man whom I had always liked and admired. He had two sons, and having spent several summers with the family many years ago, I became impressed with the way he would listen to his boys: they would get very quiet at the kitchen table and right there in that big exposed room they seemed to create an envelope of inviolable privacy. There would be nods, the touch of a huge hairy hand on a slight, growing shoulder. Laughter.

I tried it once, during a summer of unbearable loneliness and horrible feelings of incompetence. I worked at his gas station, but could never fill a tank without sloshing gas all over myself and the car, couldn't pour oil without fouling the engine block. Once, trying to fix a flat (there were no fancy machines then), I managed to push the wheel inside the tire and smashed the knuckles of my left hand in the process.

I told him what I was feeling and he took me to the kitchen table as he would one of his sons. He heard me out—and then came that hand on my shoulder. And he said, "God made us all different. You can't do what I can, and someday when you're a man you'll do what I can't. That's the way it should be. A whole bunch of grown men doing different things. Without that, where would the fun be in the world?"

Somehow, by the end of that summer, I pumped gas and poured oil, as he would say, "real good." He never *taught* me how . . .

I watched the family approach the bier one by one, pray briefly, touch his folded hands and kiss his forehead, and I did the same. Simple. A straight good-bye.

But what I remember most clearly was our return from the cemetery to his house, his oldest son taking an envelope from his breast pocket and saying, "Pop wanted me to read this. It says, 'I hope when you read this I am in a good place. I don't have any regrets, but what I could never stand was a poor funeral. I would like you all right now, and I'm not kidding about this, right now to break out the liquor and the food and get to it.' "

On the way home, on the plane, I was flooded with thoughts of my father.

He never seemed much of a father. I saw him mainly as an instrument of my mother, from whom I tried to separate, to get away from—a man whose moods hinged upon hers, happy when she was, sad when she was. A very dependent man who never seemed able to assert himself, to express himself except in the shadows of his work—which he told no one about unless he was relating an anecdote that reflected his "manliness."

If she disapproved of something, so did he—but always as if by some magic she and he arrived at the criticism independently. He could not write English very well, at least in syntax and spelling and punctuation, and neither really could she, but her errors were different. So that every time she would pen off a vitriolic missile to me, he would follow with his own—but his would be replete with *her* errors in syntax.

So I saw him as a tool. I knew he needed a mother, and she was it, and that's all it seemed to be, and that I as a son would have to suffer the loss of a father because he was weak and needed her, and that need would demolish any action he wanted to take on his own. Needing so much, he could give me close to nothing.

I remember once when I was about thirteen and she kicked him out, and I pleaded with him not to leave, to stand up to her. But all he could do was cry. And yet he also did something else, perhaps something that welled up through his fear and panic—some slight sense or feeling or even intellectual idea that he could after all be independent. He hugged me and kissed me and said he loved me and, oh Christ, what a feeling that was—the second time it had ever happened. The first time was when he came home drunk and surrounded me with his arms and tousled my hair, and I loved the smell of the old saloon on him, a smell of vaguely old whiskey that somehow I still love, although it can make other people retch. Two times: once when he was free enough in his drunkenness not to have to take responsibility for what he was doing, and then when he felt some ancient, archaic pang of the sense of freedom.

He left that day and I hated her and I wanted to go off with him and I sat in the cellar and cried and railed at her.

Two days later he came back.

He called her Mom.

She called him Daddy.

For me he was a washout.

And then came a time when we became so profoundly close for just less than a minute that I will never forget it even though it lasted no longer than the snap of one's fingers.

He became terminally ill, and my mother nursed him at home and she complained bitterly that she had cared for him all her life through all his sicknesses—yet he was never really a sick man. She complained and nagged and put him on some sort of Bismarckian regimen that almost broke his spirit. And one day he said to me, "How are you? How's everything?"

"Good. Fine."

"I'm glad," he said, and squeezed my hand. And then: "Your mother. You know, she's impossible to live with." And crying, the tears streaming down his cheeks: "I've got to get out of here, get a job, anything. I can't live with her."

The only moment of adult closeness we had ever had. And it was to be the last, not because he died soon after, but because he sank back into his need for her and again shut me out.

She called me an inspiration. The way in which I had

handled the emergencies surrounding his illness was "inspiring." She wrote that in a note to me and I still have it somewhere—because it was the only time she had ever acknowledged me as an adult with capabilities and maturity.

And then soon after I was nothing again.

He wrote me a letter condemning my life, a letter filled with *her* words, not his; filled with *her* errors of syntax, not his.

And, enraged, I broke off our relationship.

And then he died.

And as I watched him lying in his half-opened coffin in the funeral parlor, images passed through my mind of his weakness (and I could not decipher the expression on his dead face), of his domination by her and need for her (and still I could not fathom that death-look), and I could pick up her words in the background, words telling neighbors what a good man he was, how kind and considerate and loving (and damn it, that expression still would not fall into place), and I felt somehow surrounded by a fantasy, a myth, hearing words about him that were weaving themselves into a fiction, into a legend that was being built (what *was* that face saying?), and there was an absence of people in the family who had once professed so much liking for him and yet were not there to say good-bye, as if the words I was hearing had somehow erased them with unreality, as if they could not be there while the myth was being constructed . . .

And for a moment it was too much to look at, to listen to.

I walked around the room slowly and I listened to the talk again, and suddenly the words being built into the myth struck me in a different way, and then I saw. I saw that she was inventing a life for him, all the traits, characteristics, that she would want the world to see him possessing, a life she was building to suit herself, of the kind of man she was married to—and it was all a fiction, and the people who were not there, had not come, knew it to be a fiction and could not be there to see it, hear it, could not have borne it.

I cannot describe the intensity of my awareness of the conspiracy that had been built between them—that he had manipulated her as cunningly as she had manipulated him. And what had been left out of it all was their son.

He was finally becoming in public what she had always wanted him to, what he had always wanted to be.

"He was considerate to others even on the day he died. Why, when . . ."

"We had our bad times, but he was always a good provider."

"He could never stand those homosexuals on television. He was a real man, you know."

And then I stared at his face. And I saw it.

Wreathed by the soft satin of his pillow and by the halo of red and white roses was an expression of an almost awesome smugness.

Finally, in death, emerged the expression of what he had always been.

Smug.

My mother was saying, "He would stand up to anybody. I remember one time . . ."

I couldn't remember it at all.

SIX

THE MAKING OF A MACHO

I have used the term "demythologize" in a number of places throughout this book, and it means an attempt to puncture not those myths which enhance our living—like the journeys of heroines and heroes into the depths of their beings to discover inner truth—but to take many stereotypes, fairy stories if you will, and turn them on end. Not to pro claim that anyone has any sort of ultimate truth, but to stimulate different ways of looking at phenomena and happenings and situations that have been taken for granted because of our incredibly simplistic ideas about cause and effect.

For example, an unfortunately common cliché: boys become invested with machismo, with sexism, with the stereotypical social masculine role because they model themselves on fathers who themselves are macho, sexists, oppressors of women. In this superficial view of things, the boy watches his father behave like a sexist, watches him put down his mother and treat his sister like some hysterical little powerless doll—and thereby begins to evolve his own self-image of a dominating, powerful male. If true, this formula would explain everything. But at best it is only a partial truth and can only be true in very circumscribed social contexts. And it dismisses the mother entirely.

Observers seeking a more balanced perspective frequently contribute the idea that, in some way not clearly definable, mother *must* have something to do with this "masculine evolution" and role assumption. But what? What does she *do?* What does she convey? In what ways does she collude, if collude she does?

Let's first eavesdrop on an encounter between the writer and a sensitive, dedicated feminist, a psychotherapist. In this brief dialogue there is an important issue that rises to the surface, namely, the frustrating search for ultimate causes and ultimate responsibility—a search that is always on the verge of breaking down into seemingly simplistic elements.

PAULA: It's very hard for me to see how a boy can grow up to be a typical sexist without being mostly influenced by his father.

PAUL: But not by mother?

PAULA: Oh, yes, sure. And I grapple with that issue because when I'm in sessions with my patients I see so many complexities, so many cross-currents. But there's so much of a modeling effect gotten from exposure to fathers.

PAUL: Tell me what you see. Obviously I get exposed to men who need to show me how masculine they are, but it's mostly along lines of competition with men.

PAULA: Okay, there's often a kind of masculine primping, a holding up of the posture, often a subtle putdown of my credentials and qualifications.

PAUL: Like?

PAULA: "Oh, you have a Ph.D.? I was under the impression that most female shrinks were social workers." Like that. Or: "You have a Ph.D.? In what?" Then there's the obvious flirtatiousness, the immediate use of my first name, the ending of sessions with something like, "Same time, same place, Paula?"

PAUL: You see the anxiety there.

PAULA: Oh, yes, the inability to relate to a woman except through the pose of superiority.

PAUL: But it's unpleasant.

PAULA: I could grit my teeth.

PAUL: You think it's all modeling? You don't feel that there has to be some subtle—maybe even not so subtle—push in that direction by the mother?

PAULA: There must be, of course. There are some studies showing that mothers treat their male and female children very differently—that boys are allowed more freedom, more activity, and all of that. But I think that where this situation exists, you'll find that the mothers have been so bamboozled and influenced by a male-dominated society that they just perpetuate what they've been told—what they've been conditioned by. Most of them don't even know they're doing it.

PAUL: Isn't it also possible that women have internal images of men, deep internal fantasies about men that they mold their sons into?

PAULA: Sure, but wouldn't those fantasies simply

be derivatives of living in a culture dominated by
men?

PAUL: There was a time when many cultures were
dominated by women. There's an interesting thing
I've jotted down. You know the book *The First Sex*,
by Elizabeth Gould Davis?

PAULA: Yes.

PAUL: Well, on the cover of the paperback edition
is a very peculiar statement. It says, "Ancient civiliza-
tions such as the Sumerian were matriarchal societies
where women ruled and men were servants. . . . The
collapse of these matriarchal societies signaled the
brutalization of humanity and the increased suppres-
sion of women . . ." I find this a very weird statement: men were servants and the societies were not
brutal; women became servants and the societies became brutal.

PAULA: Put that way, of course it's weird. There's
no balance in it.

PAUL: Could there be something in the wind like
so: If women were once dominant, it certainly means
that women can *be* dominant—and many certainly are
these days, and more will be, in business, government,
whatever. But that dominance for these outgoing,
assertive women isn't particularly a "male" thing,
whereas for most women, who are housewives and
mothers, dominance is still the province of the male,
and since they cannot or have chosen not to participate in the larger world, they act out that dominance,
what they see as maleness, through their male children. In other words, *he* will become the "man"
I wish I was. He will become the man of my dreams—

myself or the real man I should have become involved
with.

PAULA: I guess that's very possible.

PAUL: And that the father may have very little to
do with it? In fact, he might not even be aware of
what's going on?

PAULA: You're dealing with human behavior. So
anything's possible.

PAUL: Okay, flat out: Could a man get to be a
macho, a sexist, *mainly* through the influence of his
mother?

PAULA: I find that very hard to get with.

PAUL: Or did most men get to be the way they are
because societies were once matriarchal?

PAULA: Do we need this?

PAUL: I wish we didn't—but all these causes and
blames seem to be the backbone of all kinds of angry
and defensive debates on the part of men and women.

PAULA: Look, I don't think we'll ever get to the
roots of all this, although I wish we could. We'd be
better off if we just acknowledge what *is*, forget the
blames and the historical search and stick with now.

PAUL: Amen.

SKETCHES FROM A PLAYGROUND

I was sitting in a playground one spring afternoon—a playground I very often go to with my children because it's
grassy, cool, and filled with swings, monkeybars, and nifty
animals set on springs. Also hopscotch squares, a sometimes
violent miniature hand-turned merry-go-round, and seesaws.
You can also play whiffleball there, and it's always a place
where we seem to laugh a lot and take instant refuge from

the Mister Softee truck which needs a new tape of its vaguely moronic song.

The playground is also a microcosm. And perhaps that is also why we—subliminally—are attracted to it.

I was sitting there on this particular day becoming interested in a woman who began to scream at a group of boys, accusing them of stealing a ball. They looked puzzled and offended, and one of the boys tossed the ball toward her and said, "It was just lying here." But she kept on for a few minutes and they edged from discomfort into a sort of sulky anger, and when she stopped they shrugged, turned away, and got involved with themselves again.

The woman went to the far end of the playground, sat on a bench, and seemed to be interested in nothing much in particular. In fact she seemed to be alone, not attached to any of the children. Suddenly she shouted something inarticulate and brief, and I noticed that a small boy jerked his head toward her, and I assumed he was hers. He was quite small, about seven years old, and was huddled over a baseball glove and a bat talking to another boy roughly his own size and age. After a few minutes whatever they were doing so quietly in their huddle burst apart as if they had stepped on a land mine.

They squared off. It reminded me of very violent confrontations—from *On the Waterfront* or a Charles Bronson movie—and not at all like the cowboy-type encounters from our childhoods. It was a bit scary, Vietnamish, the low crouches, the hands loose, the odd jungle postures, and very mean, almost evil faces—and they weren't much like little boys any longer, especially the boy I took to be the woman's child.

He hit first, a long, looping adult uppercut that caught the other boy on the side of his head. And for me, that was it. I was ready to break it up on the spot; it looked just too vicious, too serious, almost deadly. As I got up, the woman left her bench and walked toward the boys, then stopped and watched with her hands on her hips.

The boy who was hit swung back and contacted only a shoulder, and the first boy shot a vicious kick into his shins, then slammed him down on his stomach, wedged his forearm against his throat, and began to pull back.

A murder?

As I jumped up, the other boy's friends (the ones the woman had yelled at about the ball) raced across the grass and quickly broke it up. But the woman merely stood, hands still on hips, watching.

She gave me the creeps. And so did her kid.

With the fight broken up, the obviously beaten kid joined the group, and as his friends were comforting him— he was crying by this time—the woman joined her son and together they walked past the group of boys on their way out of the playground. Suddenly she turned and said something to them, one of the boys replied, and she said something again. And then something happened which is very rare: the largest boy in the group turned crimson, clenched his fists, and stepped out toward her. How often do you see a boy of about eleven pushed so far over a line that he instinctively steps forward toward an adult woman?

But he recovered, draw back, and merely glowered. The woman's son snapped something at him, but by this time he had managed to establish control and he didn't respond.

The mother and son left the playground walking slowly —strolling actually—and as they walked out and along the sidewalk she dropped back a few paces and walked behind him. He was not walking quickly or bounding ahead as kids will do. She just dropped behind him like some subservient

Japanese woman from another century as he walked on with his baseball bat perched jauntily on his shoulder.

First, let's merely *see* what happened here.

A mother accuses a group of boys of stealing. She moves away to the farthest reaches of the playground. Her small son becomes involved in a fight serious enough to upset and vaguely frighten an adult observer. The mother approaches and watches as her son seems almost ready to kill his opponent. She says and does nothing. A group of boys are concerned enough to break up the fight even though the two boys are similar in age and size. The mother leaves with her son. She says something to the boys. One boy appears angry enough to want to attack her. Her son says something. They leave, the mother walking behind the son.

Now let's let ourselves go with some possible interpretions of what we've observed. Let's get into the larger world-view of this microcosm and see the making of a macho.

The woman approaches a group of boys—a man's world—and accuses them of stealing something; in other words, the man's world has stolen something (from her) and she feels deprived by the "theft," adopting a belligerent and somewhat paranoid stance toward it. She appears to be alone, isolated, removed from this world, and as if to underline the point, she moves off into the isolation of a bench in the far corner of the playground—in the far corner of the space, the world, in which she lives.

Suddenly she hollers something unintelligible and it becomes clear that she is after all linked to one of the "men" (her small boy), and perhaps her cry (only "perhaps" because what she says isn't clear) mobilizes something inside the boy. Or perhaps the other boy has made some comment on the mother's action. There is a moment of quiet followed by an eruption of the boy's anger or combativeness. He faces his enemy like a Green Beret facing a Vietcong, and begins to work him over with such ferocity that he almost strangles him.

The mother has come forth from her isolation to watch the mayhem, and despite the sheer brutality of it, the possibility of serious injury, she does nothing but watch with her hands rolled into fists on her hips.

The other boys rush over, and it becomes clear that the endangered boy is a member of their group—the group accused of having stolen the ball. Does she know this? That this choking little boy is a member of the man's world represented in the playground by a particular group of children—or is she satisfied that he is merely a member of a race of men whom she finds depriving and attacking?

But what *is* clear is that her son is engaged in killing off one of the men she accuses, probably hates. He is being violent for her; he is killing for her.

He is protecting her honor.

He is her knight, her courtly lover, and he is waving her banner.

And there is little doubt that he is not at all aware of what he is doing.

And in all probability neither is she.

But she likes what she sees. She doesn't stop it. What happens to the boy who is being choked is of no concern to her. He deserves it. She is watching her hero in action. St. George and the dragon; Siegfried slaying Fafner the serpent; Odysseus, Ivanhoe, and all the rest.

Except that these are seven-year-old boys and she is a grown woman.

And then as they leave she hurls what looks like a vicious taunt at the group of boys, leaving no room for chivalry—taunts the world of men, giving them no opportunity to do anything but attack her. And by that act, by almost provoking a boy-man into the unthinkable act of attacking a woman, she renews her proof that the world of men is violent and brutal. For what sort of men attack a woman? Apparently all men—except one.

And he hurls one last taunt of his own—at the world of men—and walks off with his symbol of masculinity across his shoulder, and she then walks off behind him, the woman subservient to her powerful man, the *most* powerful man, and clearly superior to all of them, and clearly *hers*. Her man.

Basking in the fantasy of having given birth to the hero, she walks behind him. Behind the Man.

She has made a macho. A sexist. Not only in her molding him into her fighter, but in walking behind him. She is giving him the illusion that he is not only superior to other men, but that as a man he is superior even to her.

Of course we can speculate on the role of the boy's father—but he is not there, he is not in the playground on a spring afternoon with his son. Where is he? Home watching the Yankees? Washing the car? Moonlighting for a few extra dollars? Is he anywhere? And does it matter?

Where he is emotionally for her is probably in that world of men that she dislikes, taunts, loathes, and attacks through her son.

And anyway, how could he ever match up to her hero?

I am watching the kids whirling around on that demonic, dervish-like disk of a merry-go-round, and notice that one boy of about four whom we have known since he was an infant is wearing a patch on his eye.

"What happened to Richie?" I ask his mother.

"What a mess," she says. "That damn nursery school has no supervision at all sometimes. I'm almost ready to pull him out of it."

"He had an accident?"

"Yes and no. He was horsing around with another boy in the sandbox, throwing sand at each other, and the other kid threw a whole handful in his face. A pound of it must have landed in his eye."

"Why the patch?"

"Abrasions or something. We took him to the emergency room as fast as we could."

"That happened to me when I was a kid, but I cried most of it out. Didn't Richie cry?"

"Cry? Why should he cry?"

I feel uneasily perched on the forbidden territory of one woman's child-raising techniques.

"Why not? It hurts."

"Do you think he'd cry in front of *him*?"

"In front of who?"

"The director of that lousy nursery school, that's who." Her nostrils flare. "He'd never cry in front of *him*."

This is not a woman who ever gives an impression that she dislikes men. Certainly she dislikes the director of the nursey school, and certainly her dislike has a strong element of competition in it, because she is so very proud that her son acted "manly." Abrasions or not, patch or not, he didn't cry. Ergo a man.

"What's he like—the director?"

"Kind of smart-assy. A know-it-all. Not really faggy, but effeminate—well, affected. You have a question, *he's* got the answer. Nothing you do is right—especially the way you raise your kids. All the mothers complain about him—but they have the best facilities for kids of any of the schools."

Without any awareness whatever, she has just described her husband, whom I know slightly. Although he is clearly affected, he is not effeminate; he is prissy. But does she have some unspoken, perhaps even unconscious, doubts about his masculinity? He carps at her: this I've seen. An accountant, he has become somewhat of an amateur child psychologist ever since his son was born, and at times quotes all sorts of people at her, heavyweight psychoanalysts like Margaret Mahler, René Spitz—none of your common Spocks or Gesells.

They haven't had a good marriage. It seems clear that she wants a different kind of man—a man that fits her inner image of what a man should be.

She is in the process of forging one.

There is some kind of family picnic going on, but it looks more like an orgy of eating. With a little imagination you could conjure up a pig roasting on a spit. The family is dreadfully obese—youngish men and women and their children, all drastically overweight. Two of the men are catching a softball and after a while it is clear that they won't let their sons get in on the game. One of the men throws very high and wide and the ball sails over a low stone wall into the creek bed beyond. They send one of the boys for the ball but, too fat to scamper over the wall, he runs a distance and passes through the gate, around a Cyclone fence, and then scrambles down the embankment. Happily, he tosses the ball back but he can't get back up the embankment: he is simply too fat, too awkward.

This concerns the mother now; she is vaguely panicked, as if her son will have to remain in the creek bed forever, ritually buried like King Tut. The father, who obviously doesn't want to go around the Cyclone fence and pull the boy out, is shouting at him to climb out. He tries but can't. Every time he tries the mother becomes more hysterical and warns him not to hurt himself, not to bruise his knees or cut his hands. He hangs there on the wall a bit like a sad grape on a vine. Damned if he does, damned if he doesn't —but in actuality he *can't*.

The scene is some kind of parody.

But now my attention is taken up by another boy in the creek bed, who has been collecting bits of broken glass from the shallow bottom, polished and made smooth by the slowly flowing water. He is far younger and far smaller than his hapless peer. *His* mother is standing up on the embankment shaking her head disgustedly, disapproving of the whole scene. Fair enough. But then she says, "Lennie, show the poor little fat boy how a real boy can climb."

That is what she says.

The "real boy" almost bounds out of the creek bed, free and clear, and his mother pats his head. He is smaller, but strong, and he extends his hand toward the "poor little fat boy"—and very calmly his mother draws back his hand. He drops back into the creek bed, resumes his collecting, pays no further attention to the other boy until half the family comes to pull him out. "What's the matter with him?" he says to his mother. "Is he a boy or a girl?"

The playground. Sometimes there is play. Often there is not.

Within every woman there lives the image of a man, as within every man there lives an image of a woman. Or

Man. Or Woman. This is the inner matrix upon which is formed every relationship—for without that inner image there would be no lovers, no marriages. Yet *with* that image also comes disappointment, breakup, divorce—and, in the extreme instance, the absolute impossibility of forming any meaningful relationship at all. Very often a woman's inner image of a man is so powerful, so idealized, so blown out of any semblance of what is possible in the world, that no man can match it—and consequently all men are rejected. Then a woman finds herself in the despairing and untenable position of seeing herself as a sort of freak, an impossibility: she has been born in a time, a place, in which there are no good men at all.

But we are concerned now with an idealized internal image that becomes played out in the external world, the world of mundane practical "reality"—of an external "reality" that has as its counterpart or polar opposite the internal "reality."

The internal image is a given; it is there, built from an amalgam of everything a woman has learned from her parents, from books, movies, television; what she needs to fulfill her needs and wishes; even from the deep archetypes in the human psyche that cut across centuries and cultures. There is this *ideal* man living within—and it continues to live within even if the world of men is excoriated. Not a negative internal image of the man—I am not dealing with that here, because that can be so powerfully distorting it can wreck one's life. But the *ideal image.*

Thus is the image of the inner man created: in little girls raised and nurtured on fairy tales which later flower into "women's magazines"—the Grimm sisters of our times; in girls who are exposed to poisonous images of men and who then must detoxify by seeking healing images of men;

in the lives of the most militant feminists, whose unrelenting criticism of men implies that some more benevolent and satisfying opposite must exist.

The point is: when a mother creates and forges a macho, a stereotyped John Wayne, a sexist, *she does so out of disappointment*. And the disappointment is created by the devastation of her internal image of a man. She has brought this image, which is conscious or unconscious fantasy, to a real man—and the attempted superimposition has not worked. The picture develops fuzzy, out of focus; the colors bleed. And there is no projector that can bring the edges together into a picture of clarity and meaning.

This, of course, is what is often worked out in psychotherapy. Or at least the attempt is made to work it out.

He is not what I thought he was. He is not the same person I married.

Quite so. We marry ourselves.

This is the root, the bedrock, of passionate love. This is the stuff of which the romantic movement in art, literature, and music is made—and why it remains so popular. This is why a romantic opera, a romantic novel, often ends with the suicide of one or both of the lovers. The suicide usually occurs just at the point of recognition that the other person is different, is an individual, is not what has been made of him. Or that the other person is committed to someone else, has a separate life, other responsibilities. The other person is different, apart, has his own identity and contents of a life.

Some attraction, perhaps solely physical, perhaps intellectual, whatever, is set off when a woman meets a man. What immediately comes into play is a projection onto that man of the image of the man within—so powerfully projected if affection is returned that the real man is all but blotted out. And if the man is swept up he actually *does* lose some objective identity since he switches into a position of living only to see his beloved. If he has an identity involving his work, this identity ceases to be, at least temporarily. This is a reciprocal affair, but here we will confine our discussion to the development of this situation in the woman.

So onto this real man is projected the ideal image of the man: he is fleshed out with it, his blood runs with it, even his facial expression takes it on.

Whatever the ideal man is, whatever his components, the image is often a fatal one if it is suffused with expectations that are sought for in the external world. Because he cannot be found; he doesn't exist; he is a fairy tale. The real man cannot match up: reality is a poor substitute for fantasy.

The image of the ideal man exists even in the inner life of dedicated feminists, especially in those women who are deeply angry with men and reject them. Because the rejection of men implies that men have failed to meet a standard—a standard as unrealistic as the ideal image it is founded on. And so, failing it, men are rejected.

The inner images are many and complicated: they range from very primitive knights in armor, tall handsome virile lovers, powerful warriors (all of which appear frequently in dreams), to more subtle characters, even animals. In some women the inner images shade into nonsexual men, older, kinder, fatherlike men who will provide for them, support them, with whom they can remain little girls.

When one or more, or a mixture, of these images are projected onto a man he loses his identity as a separate person and becomes the woman's fantasied lover, the ideal man, and he will be expected to fulfill the dream.

We cannot help the development of this process in this place and time. We live in a basically unreal society whose economic life depends heavily on the perpetuation of false images—on failed romance, failed love, on fantasy. These fantasies are encouraged; truth, what is, is denied because if not, no one would buy anything useless and there would be an equality that would destroy the power bases.

The custom of the honeymoon perpetuates the fantasy—and perpetuates it in a cruel and cynical way, because it creates an unreal atmosphere against which the harshness of what follows is painfully contrasted. The plunge into the realities of daily living following this hiatus in life can be almost unbearable.

And the message is quite clear: enjoy the fantasy while you can—it's your last crack at it.

What begins to happen is that individual identities, or at least individual roles, come back into play as soon as the first rent bill, the first electric and gas bills, begin to sift into the mailbox. The man begins to focus on the necessity of striving to earn more money, to be successful, to advance himself. The woman, if she is dedicated to a career, begins to do likewise; if she remains a housewife, the long days of crushing boredom and loss of self-esteem begin to mount like storm clouds in a once clear sky. They begin to see less of each other; what happened to the honeymoon? They develop individual problems of greater proportions; seeds of discontent and unhappiness, always there, start to flower—and the long corrosive process of disenchantment and disappointment works itself into the fabric of their lives.

Neither husband nor wife understands that one's individual problems may have something to do—or even *everything* to do—with *oneself*.

This is not the man I married, says the wife.

And here is where the ideal image of the man breaks down, fragments, disintegrates—and when this happens, the tendency is not to retreat for a look inside, to wonder how the image became constructed, how it worked to distort reality, but to externalize it, to blame the man for his failure to live up to his promises. Except that in most cases no promises were ever made.

The knight falls from his horse; the banner is shredded and tattered.

When this occurs, when all is externalized, when the disappointment is taken as "objective" fact and not the result of a failed daydream, the need to find the inner man continues to press, continues to torment—and an affair may result, always looking for that man somewhere *out there*. It rarely works.

There may be a child. A boy child.

This boy child may then become the substitute for the husband—the living flesh out of which the ideal man will be created; and, in pulling the child away from the influence of the father—who is anyway too preoccupied with his own concerns—the mother will build, layer by layer, the ideal man. *Her* man. The man who will never disappoint her, the man who will embody in thought, word, and deed all that a man should be—a man who will also be her child. A man to the world, but *hers*, her creation, her fiction, her poem. As man he will accrue glory to her; as child he will always be dependent upon her and so she will never lose him. And she "knows" what a man is.

"Do you think he'd cry in front of *him?*"

"Lennie, show the poor little fat boy how a real boy can climb."

And "made" a "man" by his mother, the boy as man will always need to validate his manhood through women.

He is stronger than his father, more manly than his father—because she has made him so. And although he may later in life be anxious in the presence of certain men he perceives as really more powerful, he will have a certain kind of arrogance that will get him through. But he will need women for support and comfort, women who will make him *feel* like a man. He will become a sexually dominating macho, he will need passive, clinging, dependent women—always in search of his own male identity, but never quite finding it.

He is a fictional character. He looks like a man. But he is a mirror image of something deep within his mother's being, and he is a product of disappointment—and will always be, in the guise of a man, his mother's boy.

There is a so-called health club in the lower level of a local building, and the tenants are convinced that it is really a high-class massage parlor. Watching the men enter, watching them bluff and kid, can be a fascinating pastime. On this particularly rainy night, three well-dressed men walk in, and as they prepare to descend to the pleasures of the night, one quickly removes a pocket comb and in the mirror by the elevator door makes sure that his hair is neat, his part straight.

A marvelous piece of business. Prepared to partake in a macho ritual, prepared to have himself serviced like his car, prepared to have some brief encounter with an anonymous woman whose name is Carol but who will call herself Betty or Roz, he pauses and combs his hair. It will give him courage to perform.

The elevator door slides shut. The boy-man disappears. *Down*, as Mephistopheles said to Faust: *Down to the mothers.*

By a set of fortunate circumstances a woman might conceivably be brought up relatively free of the burden of the
ideal image of a man. ("Conceivably" is not a word bred
of cynicism; I use it to reflect the confused state of the
human art.) Suppose, in a parental setting of relative har-
mony and clear vision, she is made less prone to the distorted forces that construct images of saviors and knights
in armor. What then? Then she might be blessed with a
kind of clarity that lets her see through the mirages and
fantasies and wish-fulfillments; that lets her, most assuredly,
fall in love, but in love with a *person*—a man who is less
likely to disappoint her because he is seen for what he is. A
person whose mission is not to fulfill a fantasy, but to com-
plement a life.

Free of the *inevitability* of disappointment, she will have
no need to mold a boy child into the image she needs to
find expressed in the external world.

In her independence, she will live her own life, become
her own person, and will use her inner image of *reality* to
help her boy become a person; and in bringing in the father
to help in the process, the issue then does not become the
boy as man, but the boy as person, and as developing human
being—and the sexual identity will take care of itself. In its
own way.

We may yet arrive at this point. *Why* this doesn't happen more often, *why* people must often try to work this out
in therapy—the *whys* are not terribly important at this
point. Because in our way of looking for blame, we will get
less to cause than to accusation. To blame men for creating
a world in which this happens, to accuse women of doing
the same—both are circular and fruitless positions and both
avoid seeing the situation as it exists, as it is. Otherwise,

both sexes will attribute enormous power to the other—a power that neither has.

And then we will enter the arena of male–female politics, and politics is a smokescreen covering the necessity to achieve a personal inner balance.

SEVEN
LEAVING HOME

The playground; school; work and perhaps marriage: time moves on for the son, and until he reaches some stage of adulthood he will not have much sense or awareness of the movement. But the passage of time is opening possibilities for him. As he grows, things are happening, the future seems built in to the now. He is an actor in the action of the outside world. He is involved in it, part of it, flexing his muscles.

And he is headed for conflict. He is his mother's son, he lives with her, and yet for a time he is going to forget that fact, so involved is he with the larger world, so enamored of the idea of approaching manhood. He knows he is growing toward independence, and so he may "put up" with the rules of the household, express annoyance with strictures placed on his adolescent years. He can bear with it: one day he will be gone and nobody will be able to tell him what to do.

He is definitely headed for conflict.

Because for the mother, unlike her son, time is beginning to close in; it is not opening new possibilities, new explorations. And this is especially true if she has spent the bulk of her years living for and through her son. As he grows she may take pride in his accomplishments, in what he is doing. But all the while she is confronted with the alien, even frightening, fact that he is growing up, looking more like a man, and she begins to realize that one day he will leave her.

The conflict will become apparent, will mushroom, when the decision to leave has been made and the necessary confrontation occurs. And occur it will, and the son will suddenly realize that it is not his desire alone, not his growth alone, that is propelling him away from home; his desire is not enough in itself. He realizes that he must cope with his mother's reaction, and that whatever decision he makes will be heavily influenced by what pressures she brings to the situation.

He wishes to leave. She wants him to stay. The battle lines are drawn around these opposite feelings.

This is a crucial confrontation for mother and son, and the shock of it is sometimes shattering and depressing for both of them. And the conflict may appear to be entirely irrational, with a host of facts overlooked, even denied, and this denial can be painfully confusing for a son. After all, his growing up has certainly been noticed by his mother. Hasn't he grown taller, hairier, hasn't he learned to drive, to manage money to some extent? Hasn't his voice deepened? Why, then, is she challenging his right to grow up fully and leave the nest?

He must cope with this, suffer with this; it can be a blow
to him, as if a rug were pulled out from under his feet.
What in God's name is she trying to do?

And indeed, the mother seems to have taken leave of
her senses, refusing to perceive anything in grown-up terms.
She is again relating to him as if he were a child and she
the powerful mother. Remember that while external situations change, no matter how dramatically, the internal images remain essentially the same: there is the all-powerful
mother and the dependent child—and as long as they live
together this basic, primal relationship is going to remain
dominant. And at moments of crisis, such as the impending
departure of the son, the mother will revert almost mani-
acally to this deep and ancient bond. She will invoke it, and
a son will have to recognize that and deal with it; he may
have to soothe her away from it, even break it angrily. But
he must know that it is there.

It is going to be played out, but with the son no longer
reduced to helplessness. She will try to return him to his
childhood so that he will heed her and fear her displeasure,
and to some extent her pressure will cause him to retreat.
He will often *feel* like a little boy in the confrontation,
seeing her as a controlling force from which he must free
himself. And often this conflict will work for the son: the
mother is behaving *openly* now, illustrating the very needs
for control and domination that caused him, in his development from boy to man, to feel the need to leave her, to
want to leave her.

Frequently she will grasp desperately. In reaction he will
attempt to pry her fingers from his psyche.

Though the conflict may be played out with great intensity, it need not always be expressed by anger; there do

not have to be explosions in the household on a regular basis. Fights do not have to occur every day. Very often the intensity exists below the surface, and both mother and son attempt to cope with the situation on a less dramatic level —at least behaviorally. They may talk about it—and the conflict may achieve a kind of subtlety.

The subtlety here is that both mother and son must often play a game: How can they both play at independence from each other while maintaining their bond? The bond that runs so deep and that they have both needed so badly. And what happens when the bond of *physical* nearness, of daily closeness, snaps?

At first the severing of the physical bond brings with it fears that the emotional bond will snap as well; the inner is very often confused with the outer, the emotional with the purely physical, and there is a tendency in all of us to worry that a physical separation signifies the end of a relationship. And very often it can; except with mother. But even then it may take some time, some regrouping, to realize that the internal bond is hardly affected at all.

The preamble to the son's physical move can be stormy and often is, and the mother wants to know the answers to certain questions, asking them plaintively and sometimes demandingly, and they are loosely as follows:

"Aren't you too young to think of moving out?"

"Why are you pulling away from us?"

"How will you make out?"

"Can't you stay home until you get everything straighter in your mind?"

And, I have heard, "Don't you love me anymore? What have I done?"

There is an edge of panic in all of these questions, a

great deal of anger in some of them. But the message is as clear as it can be: "Don't leave. Please don't leave. It isn't time yet, not for me."

A mother's attitudes and feelings here are vastly different when dealing with a son than when dealing with a daughter. Time after time one hears mothers accusing their daughters of wanting to leave home in order to have sexual experiences. And they project other fears in their identification with their daughters as females: the fear of living alone, the fear of rape, of mugging, the fear of an independence asserted, an independence of which the mother has not been capable or has felt herself too trapped to take.

With a son it is vastly different, because the focus is almost entirely upon *losing* the son, mother losing her man, mother losing her boy. As one mother said with rancor, "I did everything for him, gave him the best of everything, worked for him—and now he's leaving me. What was it all for?"

That of course is a rather stark statement, but it lurks beneath the surface of many mothers who might not be fully aware of the sentiment or who, if they *are* aware of it, feel a sense of shame in admitting to it.

But it plays out, and plays out strongly. What is going to happen to my creation? I've molded and crafted this creation and now it is going to be taken from me, it is going to leave me. It is as if Tolstoy had lost his only manuscript copy of *War and Peace*. But a mother, at this new and strange point in her life, may not be able to craft a new creation. She can only experience loss.

A son (like a daughter) can effect the physical separation in roughly two ways: he can marry straight from his parental home, or he can move out and live alone before he decides to marry or remain single. In either case this process is to some degree a torture for the mother. Society, with its propensity for replacing human feeling and response with abstractions, purports to support male independence and pretends that because it is "normative," its achievement should cause no pain. And the mother receives no support at all for her inner hurt and resistance. She is stuck with her reactions, and though the expression of them may be muted, the pain of her loss is no less acute.

The sharpest reaction in my experience, and in the experiences of acquaintances and clients, occurs when a son just plain leaves home with no other purpose than to live by himself. The question of *why* he would want to do this becomes the key question, the obsessive question: his departure with no other purpose but to be by himself implies a striking rejection, a turning of his back on everything he has been, on everything he has related to. One man describes it this way:

> I don't think I'll ever be able to convince my mother that my wish to leave home and take my own apartment was anything but a slap in her face. We talked about it, sometimes we ranted about it, but I couldn't make clear that I felt this need to make my own way in the world, to find out who I was away from the nest. That I didn't want to be taken care of anymore, that I wanted to see what it would be like to try to grow up.
>
> She always expressed it as either some failing on her part or some hatred of her on my part. She was never able to understand that it might have been because of something positive between us that I had the guts to do it. As a matter of fact, she found *that* an absolutely ridiculous statement on my part and

thought I was patronizing her. I think her final resolution was: "Nobody wants to live alone. And if you want to live alone so badly there must be something horribly wrong."

And that's sort of where we left it. And for a long while after that, whenever I'd come over to have supper or just to visit for a while, she would kind of look at me intensely, scrutinizing, as if she couldn't believe that I could be feeling good about myself, or that I'd shaved, or that I wasn't starving. I'm not sure she can get with it yet, and it's been years.

There is a story within this story: she cannot believe that as a man, living alone, without her, he can be happy, can take care of himself. Even that he can shave or dress well or not starve. And she cannot accept that he can do all these things with no great difficulty because in some way she has provided a context of independence for him to do them in.

She simply cannot understand how he can make it without her. There is obviously some feeling within her of great confusion: How in God's name is he able to care for himself without me? And hence I am now useless, I have no function, no meaning—I am getting old and useless and perhaps on the way down the road to death.

All these separations between mother and son have this in common: it is like the moment of truth in a bullring where the abyss of mortality opens wide and one is aware that time is coming to an end. *I can die.* Which is really contained in the at times overwhelming sense that I, mother, am old now, am useless now, and the world is spinning away from me, and it can get along without me. *I am going to die.*

This is an entirely natural feeling: it cannot be otherwise after having spent year after year so closely bonded physically, pouring so much energy and time into the creation that in some way, again like a great work of art, is supposed to last forever, timeless, a product which guarantees the creator a cloak of immortality.

Being natural, then, the separation will bring with it a kind of expected depression, a sense of loss, and the need to mourn, to grieve; and being natural, the pain will eventually lessen, something learned, and the relationship may go on along different lines, perhaps on what we have come to call a more mature level. And if the mother is truly sensitive to herself, she will one day come to see that the internal bond is actually not damaged at all, that it remains intact in essentially the same way.

It is the mother who has no, or very little, sensitivity to her inner life who takes the physical separation as an insurmountable loss, a devastating blow. She cannot understand that by letting her son go she can guarantee that she will still have him. And so begins a variety of desperate grasping maneuvers, unrelenting criticisms—so many of which we've seen illustrated in these pages.

In essence, it is the mother who must separate from the son—not only the son who must separate from the mother. Both must seize the opportunity to grow, but it takes a lot of doing because the gulf between them can seem so vast, so unbridgeable. Simply because of this: the son has his life ahead of him and recognizes the need to grow (however he defines that term), to become something, and since he is in the process of that experience himself, the orientation is action, movement, without any *particular* set of thoughts about it. He is engaged in his own movement and because of that preoccupation with self, the movement is largely reflexive.

Mother, conversely, has a sense that she has already grown (however *she* defines that term), that, as most adults feel in our culture, she *has* grown up, *has* gotten somewhere, is in some sense complete because she has spun out her role, done her job, and has become firmly identified with her mission and achievement. So she is *not* engaged in her own process of movement, and she thinks too much about the separation; she experiences profound pain at the contemplation of the loss of a person who has contributed in an incalculably profound way to what she has come to accept as her identity and her purpose. What she is then engaged in, as a counterpoise to her son's movement, as an antagonistic counterpoise at that, is her position of stability, of changelessness. She wants to be settled; her son is unsettled and unsettling.

This is the gulf. But it can be bridged. The mother, in the midst of suffering the emotional wrench of her son's departure, must look within her, find personal meaning and a purpose in life separate from her son's existence. She must grow up herself, give up the position of stability, face her mortality, and set her own movement back in process.

To return to a mythic motif, she is like the great mother earth—stable, unchangeable—suddenly wracked by an earthquake. Her son wishes to fly—but air is not her medium.

And I am suddenly reminded of the tarot, those beautiful and mystical cards so maligned and profaned by a host of quacks who "tell fortunes" and "advise spiritually." While a tarot deck contains many cards, there are twenty-two of them that compose what is called the major arcana. Simply and eloquently, they trace a path in the development of the individual: the first ten or so detail the ways in which we live and connect and deal with the world of external "reality"—relationships, work, worldly pursuits. And then suddenly the path changes; these worldly pursuits done, accomplished, succeeded or failed at, where do we go from here? The answer is deep inside, to craft a personal meaning and then a broader meaning and then to become as balanced and as whole a person as we can. As whole as we can be at this stage of our evolution.

It is the pivot card, called the Wheel of Fortune, that changes the path from outer to inner. What I am hinting at is that when a son leaves his mother, the personal wheel of fortune is given a violent turn—and both mother and son must go their own ways, he through the process of connecting with the world he must live on the surface of, she with the world she must go into herself to discover in its fullness. And when he is through with his course through the world, the wheel of fortune will spin again. Then it will be his turn to explore within.

The wheel is movement. And the movement within can be more exciting than the movement without—when its proper turn comes.

The other way in which a son can effect the physical separation from his mother is through marriage made straight from the parental home. This move is rarely made smoothly, even when all seems to go well: a man is confronted with an entirely new situation and he may well be flooded by emotions that are strange and perplexing. To understand why a man feels and behaves as he does in the first stages of his new marriage, why his actions seem removed from the "romantic" courtship that preceded the marriage, it is necessary to understand what he is dealing with in terms of his relationship to the primal bond with his mother.

For both son and mother, marriage is a stark event, although the starkness of it can be softened at least publicly by a flurry of pre-wedding activities. What is hidden behind the activity of choosing clothing, a place for the reception, and all the rest of it, is the feeling that the most important relationship that two people can have is about to be ended in some way. There is fear beneath the facade of dinner jackets and flowers—a fear of the unknown. What is going to happen to our closeness, to our bond which seemed so permanent, so insoluble?

Both son and mother ask this question; and the answer can only be forthcoming through immersion in the experience of the marriage itself. An enormous adjustment must be made on the part of the son—an adjustment to removing himself physically from his mother, which is, I feel, much more difficult an adjustment than learning to live with another person. While a man must of course get to know the woman he has married—even though they might have lived together for some time—he must also work through the separation from his mother.

Because the transition from mother's home to marital home is not going to be a smooth one. There will be feelings never expressed before, these usually initiated by the mother—and these must be coped with. There is often a sense of loneliness at the end of the marriage ceremony, a loneliness that extends into the honeymoon, if there is one, and a man finds himself thinking of all that his mother has said about the event and all that she has expressed nonverbally. He may find himself trying to transform his new wife into a copy of his mother; he may be short-tempered;

he may even find himself temporarily impotent as a way of hanging on to the mother/little boy bond. He may feel angry as a delayed reaction to all the scenes that preceded the marriage. Emotions may come in quick cycles: happiness, depression, anger, numbness. I have known men who became drunk on their wedding night, who quibbled unmercifully over plane tickets, who buried themselves for hours in a gambling casino in Aruba or Puerto Rico.

They were wondering not only whom they were with but whom they had left.

So what seems on the surface to be a normal, easy movement into the upper echelon of adulthood can be a dreadfully complicated situation because, though marriage is *strongly* accepted socially, it also sets up a conflict: the mother must suddenly come to cope with another woman, and the son with his mother's reactions to her.

Mothers handle this situation in a variety of ways, from an honest acceptance to the display of an array of hostile behaviors. But there is much that goes on between these poles. I have never met a man who could say that his fiancée was accepted uncritically, although the criticism varies in sharpness and subtlety. Often there are postmortems of visits to his mother's home, and the litany of criticisms is endless, ranging from barbs to gentle questions which of necessity *must* be annoying to a man.

"Her manners aren't good."

"She has pimples."

"Where did you say you met her?"

"Does she always have trouble talking?"

And on and on.

What the mother is facing, though she would be the last person to admit it except in the most "practical" terms, is the loss of her son to a woman he seems to prefer. Prefer, because the situation so frequently triggers all sorts of hidden fantasies, including sexual ones, at the sudden facing of competition with a woman who is younger. And again the mother feels old, perched on the threshold of uselessness, about to lose her position of specialness and supremacy. I think that the last is the most important: the sudden threat of becoming the second fiddle, her accustomed power and dominance and omnipotence slipping through her fingers like sand. The sands of time. And there seems no way to reverse the process.

I underline that the sexual jealousy, although often present just beneath the surface (and you are *never* going to hear that awareness articulated by a mother), is far less important than the loss of her son, her man, her creation. How to impress upon this new young woman that mother has primacy, that mother is still the most important force in her son's life? A friend recounts:

I'd brought my fiancée to my parents' house for dinner. It was the second time she had been there and just like the first visit, the atmosphere was cordial but just a little cool. After dinner I talked to my father for a while, we turned on the TV, and after some time I became aware that my mother and Helen weren't around. I assumed they were talking together.

Finally I got up and looked around, then went upstairs to see where they were. The door to my parents' bedroom was open and I could see them, my mother and Helen, sitting on the edge of the bed. Spread out were photograph albums, and as I watched I could see that my mother was not just giving her some visual briefing about family members. She was pointing out all the pictures of me as a little boy, including one large photo of me at about the age of one. The photo has a kind of dreamy expression, with the eyes raised high toward one corner of the frame. My mother was saying, "Look at this one. We always knew he was meant for the very best in life, that he was very special. Just look at that face."

There was a process going on there that I had the sudden need to end or at least try to nip in the bud. I walked into the room and said hello, and my mother didn't at all act as if she'd been interrupted. I was feeling that I had caught her in the act—*what* act, I wasn't sure of. But she went right on with it.

From the pile of stuff on the bed she took out a couple of books I hadn't seen since I was a very little kid. I couldn't believe they were still around. She'd kept them all these years.

She wasn't being emotional. She just told it but without saying a word: Helen, you may be going to marry him, but always remember that I'm his mother. The first woman in his life. And no one can ever have what we've had; and no one *will* ever have what we've had.

I didn't interrupt. I just stayed and listened and watched—and I have to confess that even though part of what she was doing was annoying, her clinging to me as a kid, part of it gave me some sort of satisfaction. I was *that* important to her.

This is the playing out of mother's dominance, her statement that she is and will remain queen, the Great Mother. And only God knows what will happen if she is thwarted or if her supremacy is denied. And of course that is why so many mothers who are about to lose their sons to marriage keep finely tuned to the behavior and attitudes of their future daughters-in-law, tuned with an unrelenting scrutiny that at times makes the young woman feel almost paranoid. What the mother is looking for are signs of a proper respect and deference, clear communications from the younger woman that indicate an acknowledgment of that position of superiority and primacy. And once this is established— if the young woman plays the game correctly—the situation becomes somewhat eased and other feelings are allowed to develop: liking, affection, perhaps one day even love.

There is, in all of this, a mother's perception of the transfer of *power*. And she is unwilling to make it—yet nevertheless sees it as inevitable. The power of the mother is being vested in the new woman. The young woman is perceived as having more power over the son; else why would he gravitate toward her and away from his own mother? And this is why, when conflict enters the triangle in a blatant and open way, with the son by necessity and choice opting for his fiancée's or his wife's position, he is confronted by statements from his mother that he has been seduced, has been brainwashed, is being controlled.

She simply cannot believe that he would *choose* another woman over her. And so the choice is seen as no choice at all, but as a seduction. The competitor is seen as some sort of sorceress who suddenly is infused with power while the mother is losing hers.

I believe that this drama is played out always, in lesser or greater decibels—but it is a conflict that all mothers must experience and through which they must pass before they can make peace with the loss they are about to undergo. Some of course do it well—those mothers who are most open to themselves and aware of themselves and understand at least on an intellectual level that their sons are setting out to carve a life of their own, that it is all socially right, psychologically necessary. The intelligence here prevails over the emotional level. It is the mothers who have little of their inner life working for them, whose needs for control and power overwhelm all else, who are not in touch with themselves—these mothers will struggle, fight, claw to keep their sons for themselves, keep them locked in the frames of their baby photographs. And they seem completely out of touch with even the social acceptability of marriage and independence.

But a mother can always say, "Of course I want my son to marry and have a home and children. But *she* is not for him."

How to fault that? It is an opinion presented as if weighted with objective fact, as if it were measured by a faultless scientific instrument.

So we have two poles of the same conflict. Bitterness and rancor and explosiveness on one end, the working through of it and the acceptance of the situation on the other end. And there seems little doubt that the more benign end rests squarely on two factors, at least two broad factors: the mother must have a sound relationship with her own husband, have enjoyed her own marriage, and must have some access to the creative forces within herself—those forces which are individual to her and have nothing to do with the choices and decisions made by her son. Without these, the battle lines become drawn and there's hell to pay.

I don't mean to suggest that the mother's need for her future daughter-in-law's respect and deference ends suddenly. There is a process of evolution involved in it all, which often extends to helping choose furnishings for the new house or apartment, or perhaps giving advice on childbearing. And from the daughter-in-law's point of view, this might all be seen as intrusions. So everything must be worked through and accepted.

No matter who the mother is, no matter what her level of awareness and consciousness, it is a rule of life that she will in her own way—blatantly or subtly, passively or actively—continue to inform her son that she is his *mother*. Not a woman from whom he has made a normal separation; not the grandmother of his children; not just a person to whom he sends a birthday card. She is his *mother*. Whether they are estranged for a time, whether or not the relationship goes on as harmoniously as a human being can hope for, she will always in some way inform him of this fact. And he will know it to be true. And with most men, if ever there arises a conflict of loyalties between his mother and his wife or lover, the inward force will pull him toward fealty to his mother, back to her world. He may resist it, compromise with it, or give in—but he will always feel it. feel the pull, the magnetism, even if he cannot articulate it at all.

The little boy will always be there, living inside, relating to his mother as he has always related to her. And this inner relationship can enhance a life, plunge a life into conflict, or at times even wreck a life. No physical move will ever put an end to it.

Till death do us part.

And even then, who can really know?

EIGHT

THE BOND AFTER DEATH

And one day she dies. One day she is no longer there.

A phone call somewhere in the night and he sits stunned for a time, in a kind of numbness, and after a while he might look through family photograph albums, seeing her in her youth holding his three-year-old hand. And as he turns the pages he sees her taking on years, bowing to time, until on the last page there is a final picture: she is old and he is no longer a child.

She is no more, and suddenly life seems a greater mystery than death, a greater unknown, and a feeling emerges that one day he, too, will be no more.

Perhaps he has seen it for months in her face, ravaged with pain; hospital rooms, IV tubes, the losing of weight that turns flesh skeletal, that brings out such new expressions that they shade into a person he has never known at all.

And he sets up the funeral, performs the rituals, accepts the condolences, hears a eulogy that oddly has nothing to do with her, sees her back into the great womb of the earth, goes home, and ponders it all. The missed moments, the way it should have been, what he didn't do, could have done, what she didn't or couldn't do. And there is grief and anger and mourning and sometimes an intense relief. He is motherless now, and he wonders what it will be like without her.

Mother is dead.

The death of a man's mother is, I believe, an almost overwhelming event. To some men it *is* an overwhelming event that may never be weathered, never be adjusted to, never accepted. These men—and they are clearly in the minority—may respond to their mother's death with severe depression (again a synonym for despair) necessitating drug therapy, even electroshock treatment, because they cease to function in the everyday world. Their relationships lose meaning, work is no longer important; one man described it as "all the colors draining from the world"—and he meant it literally, not metaphorically. Some men respond to no therapies at all, remaining depressed for the rest of their lives, and in rare instances the death of a mother results in suicide or a suicide attempt.

I am not going to focus on the difficulties of these men; they are suffering from what we have come to call "pathological" reactions to the loss of their mothers, the results of an almost morbid dependency. The internal process seems to read: I am my mother; my mother is me; since she is dead, so am I.

Consistent with all I have been dealing with in this book, we will be most concerned with the less dramatic reactions to the event—the reactions we see *most* frequently, puzzling though they may be at times. A man whose relationship with his mother in life was not markedly damaged is going to experience a variety of feelings at her loss. He will react to it internally and often externally in behavior. Sometimes he will confuse himself, sometimes he will be largely aware of what is going on. But always he will have to cope. And I am going to focus on *how* he copes, what he sees and feels, what he confronts—both within and without.

The severely depressed man is in many ways, with a kind of self-destructive determination, keeping his mother alive within himself. But even without this terror-inspired determination, most men will find that she *does* continue to live on within, and some sort of peace must be made with that rather awesome discovery. "Out of sight, out of mind": the old adage has no meaning at all when a mother dies, and no amount of forced logic will make it so.

What lives on inside cannot die. Nor, perhaps, *should* it die.

Let's look at a man's continuing relationship with the mother who lives on within.

When she dies, at first there may be some sense of illusory freedom, then after a time no sense of freedom at all. And as time passes the man begins to recognize that his mother lives on inside of him as powerfully as ever—then realizes, if he *can*, that in a profound way nothing very much has been altered except that the physical presence *out there* is gone. And the experience of this can be almost uncanny: she is *still here*, and no amount of mourning, no cathartic explosion, is going to significantly alter the *internal* image of her. At least not in the beginning.

A man can say good-bye to the physical remains of his mother. He can touch her lifeless hands, even kiss the cold forehead, and he can cry for the loss. But the internal image of her, everything good about her and everything bad, will continue to exist as it always has. The inner image will never die; time will alter it only slightly. The death in the physical world will do nothing to change the mother who lives within. *The event itself* will not knell the death of the image.

As a man cannot divorce his mother, he cannot let her die inside him. Because she will not die. And there is nothing he can do about it.

I woke up one morning a few days after she died, and realized that I'd been dreaming about her, and it shocked me. Somehow I thought it was all over, she was gone for good, gone from life, gone from dreams —coming to see really how silly that thought was, yet believing it. Maybe wanting to believe it.

She's been dead for several years now. I no longer think, "Oh, it's Friday, dinner with Mom tonight," or "I haven't called in a week." *That's* gone. I know she's not alive and well at home, and the reflexive responses to her presence have all but completely faded away. But she's very much in my dreams—young, old, laughing with me, punishing me, whatever—all the same things I used to dream about, the same things that very often happened, all the ways she was when she was alive. Whatever I didn't understand about her before, I still don't understand. She's just as clear, or just as foggy. Or I am.

I still have a mother. Isn't that a hell of a thing? It goes on inside as it did outside. I haven't really lost her at all. Death isn't as final as I once thought.

But another man has difficulties. He is upset.

Why the hell can't she just die and leave me alone? In my dreams she's the same way she always was—criticizing, butting in, demeaning me, making me feel bad. She has the same expressions—looking down her nose, shaking her head—and I do the same things I've always done. Asking her to approve of me, accept me. And it never happens. It never happened when she was alive and it never happens now that she's dead. Why can't she get off my back for once?

Nothing has changed. *But nothing.* She might as well still be alive.

For that man, if he stays as he is, nothing will ever be softened in his dreams because nothing was ever softened in his living relationship with his mother; nothing about his perception of her, his reaction to her, has ever changed. He explores his relationship with her as little now as he did when she was alive. And so the relationship goes on within as it went on when she lived and breathed—as if there had been no death at all. Unlike the first man, who can focus on something positive and nourishing, he still feels trapped, still addresses his dream images of her as he did his living mother when he was a child, an adolescent, a man: Why can't she get off my back for once?

His waking fantasies about her also remain the same. He continues to blame her for the unhappiness of his life—and if he needs this blame to justify himself, none of it may ever change, even if he works with a sensitive therapist. It will all depend on how badly he continues to need her as a scapegoat, a whipping-woman, the bad mother; it will all depend on whether he can ever come to see that she might have given him something after all. He needs her—and needs her to be as she was for him in life: an ossified image. Just as the first man, with his more benign feelings, his more rounded and balanced relationship with his mother, still needs her: "I haven't really lost her at all." And more than needs her, *wants* her—wants to maintain the sense that a decent mother is alive within. He need never feel bereft, abandoned. Apparently he has made his peace.

A man will conduct, or attempt to conduct, much of his life in exactly the same way after his mother is dead. Because without her he feels cut off, abandoned, perhaps to some extent even dead himself. Or if not dead, then empty, frightened. He stands alone as a sole survivor, with no one to rely upon—for good or ill.

The death cannot alter the inner effects of all the years of the real relationship, especially the bond of the early years. Again, nothing that has led to the formation of the interior relationship will change *of itself*. There will be no sense of a lasting liberation that will lead to choosing a lover or wife free of the aspects of the good or bad mother. For some men there will be no less guilt in not making a duty call even though there is no one there to pick up the phone. There will be no loosening *automatically*, because of her death, of the effects of the bond that play out in so many ways. It is like a nonreligious Hindu who still cannot stand the smell of cooking meat, who almost gags at the sight of another person wolfing down a hamburger. Or a man so taken with beautiful images that he must pause at the windows of art galleries even though he knows he will be late for work. It is all that emotional, that ingrained, that strong.

My mother would never let me eat a soft pretzel when I was a kid. You know the kind: big, salty, they sell

them at umbrella stands and in the subway. She used
to tell me that they were made from horrible junk
by degenerates who spat in the dough. I always wanted
one, but I never actually went out and bought one.
After she died, I was passing this umbrella stand and
I thought I would just finally buy one—but I couldn't.
I couldn't at all. Instead of seeing a pretzel, all I
could see was an image of her warning me and preach-
ing disease. I simply couldn't bring myself to buy the
bloody thing.

The story is trivial only if one stays on the superficial
level of a man engaged with the problem of buying or not
buying a pretzel. But the implications of the problem are
far-reaching. What *more* can't he do? What else is he
stopped from doing in his life because of the warning,
ominous image of his mother? Conversely, because all these
prohibitions need balancing, what was there in the relationship that *allows* him to do what he feels is good for him?
He can't buy a pretzel but perhaps he writes beautiful short
stories or is capable of a deep love. But that is the sticking
point; because as I've pointed out before, we are far more
tuned in to what stops us, what makes us unhappy, than
we are to what makes us feel sound.

If a man wishes to free himself as best he can from his
mother's dominating influence and from attitudes toward
her which keep him dominated, if he is to emerge from his
childish conditioned state, his dependency on her, he must
work it out after she is dead *exactly as if she were still alive.*

Because she *is* still alive. Inside him, where the process
of change and true understanding takes place. A man does
not, indeed cannot, set out to free himself from, or to understand, the mother of his adult years; the stage is set years

earlier, in the relationship of the dependent boy to the all-powerful mother, the Great Goddess. So that on this most important level, a mother's physical death is irrelevant to the inner life and what takes place there.

Through whatever process of self-exploration he may undertake, the inner relationship may well change, even the dream images may to some extent change, the fantasy images and wishes may change. There may be a realization of the good and the bad, the ambivalence, what the mother has given him as well as what she hasn't—because the inner image, if it is to alter at all, if it is to diminish or grow in stature, will be there whether she is dead or not.

However, many men will not involve themselves in an exploratory process that may alter internal images of their dead mothers or give them fuller dimension. Men, more than women, cling to the more "rational" aspects of life and assume that, once dead, the mother is gone. They are of course aware of memories, some painful, others not, but there is little understanding that the relationship goes on within in all its essentials. Indeed, the refusal to mourn, the denial that the loss can be almost devastating, is at root an unconscious attempt to keep the old inner relationship intact. Even the process of mourning itself, which is always considered "healthy" and is in fact supported by social and religious ritual, is aimed at alleviating the loss of the real, flesh-and-blood person. But I submit that no process of mourning will alter the *internal* relationship; the process may jog it, open it up to exploration, but it will not change it.

The ongoing, troubling, disturbing effects of the internal relationship will perhaps propel a man into therapy, but will primarily take the form of comments such as "I've been depressed ever since my mother died" or "Funny things have been happening to me since she died," and in many cases there will be no conscious connecting link at all.

And many men will shy away from making a link between their behavior and feelings and the influence of their dead mothers. Some find such an exploration "sticky" and others even sense it as a betrayal. But once the exploration is launched it unfolds and progresses, with all sorts of feelings and memories, just as if the mother were a fully living presence. Dead or alive: the bond, once established, is fixed.

There will often be the same need for acceptance, for dialogue, but often with the wish that the mother were alive to take part, even though, while alive, she might not have been approachable in this way. Most men can't tell their mothers anything at all about these crucial, burning issues because the mother's own private life and urgent needs, her own needed perceptions of the world and of their relationship, will not permit her to hear what he has to say, much less accept it. So that dead or alive it will all occur inside, and peace will have to be made inside. And sometimes this realization can occur with a touch of humor:

> I can think about her sometimes, let my mind play
> with it. I can tell her what a bitch she's been and she
> doesn't holler back. Or I can say, "Thanks for lots of
> things," and I can really spell it out, even all the
> things I like about my life that she'd never understand,
> that she'd even be completely opposed to. And she
> can say, "You're welcome." She's dead, I'm still alive,
> yet we're both a little different now. Even though

she's dead. I suppose it all means that I've grown to be more accepting of myself and I don't need the critic as much.

One can see this sort of thing more clearly in dealing with men in therapy. (I wish I didn't have to keep using the therapy situation as *the* major unfolding situation, but it is one of the few places we seem to accept as a legitimate ground for insights, for working out what has "gone wrong.") Because in therapy, if the process is at all meaningful, the inner life continues to unfold, and the mother's positive and negative influences on her son's development are *experienced* as in no way changed by her death. For example, it is not at all uncommon for a man in a session to talk of his mother in the present tense; or, as one man put it: "She's very much in this room today."

Again, I have been concentrating on the inner relationship, the inner understanding, the inner change. But again it should be stressed that the physical death of a mother has a great impact on her son's behavior—and on how he speaks of her, what he will say about her, how he says it. I don't want to diminish or minimize the power of the event because in one way or another it is profoundly intense—even when its impact is denied.

I've suggested that many men do indeed deny the actual physical loss—and the stronger the denial, the more attached the man has been to his mother. Perhaps we might even call the attachment a symbiosis. There is no mourning ("After all, she was very old"; or, "I see her death as a release because she suffered so much"; or, "I'm glad to be rid of her"; or "I worked it out beforehand in my analysis"). Life *apparently* goes on in the same way: work, sex, whatever. There are no tears—only a fake masculinity, an "a man can cope" mentality, rationalizations. Life goes on. But in what way?

The variations on this theme are endless, but they are all played out in the service of keeping the attachment alive exactly as it was when the mother was alive—but with the difference that there may now be an idealization of her, she becomes the stuff of legends, and the man begins to brim over with all sorts of inexplicable behavior that comes from his dependency—and all this, of course, without looking inside at what it all means, what mother and son meant to each other.

> His mother has been dead for months, and he is driving with his wife and child on the North Shore of Long Island looking for a beach that he remembers but can't find. He drives some more, idly, back toward New York City, with a vague sense that he is lost. He cannot find a major parkway, but he keeps on driving, saying that he is sorry he's lost, but driving in a way that somehow to his wife suggests a person who knows exactly where he is going. And then he emerges onto a small highway and makes a left turn, goes on for two more blocks, and stops in front of an old Colonial-type house. He stares and for a moment his wife fears he is sick, that he may be having a heart attack. Beads of sweat creep down his temples.
>
> "What's the matter?" she asks, trying not to alarm their child.
>
> "That's my house," he says. "I grew up there."

He "knew," without knowing, exactly where he was going. And a man who "worked it out beforehand in my analysis," who tried to cope with the event before it occurred, has a devastating experience:

> I quit my job today. After fifteen years, I just quit.
> I brought a report in to Gert [a supervisor with whom he has always indicated a sound, amicable relationship] and she sort of frowned as she read it, and I thought I saw a real look of disgust on her face. She kept on reading it and kept on looking more and more disgusted, and suddenly I blurted out, "If you don't like it, why the hell don't you just say so? Why do you have to look at it like it's a piece of shit?"
> She stared at me, but I couldn't seem to stop. I told her I'd had it with her, had had it for years, and that she could take the job and shove it. And I walked out.
> What did I do? Jesus, what did I do? I must have gone crazy.

He didn't go crazy at all. Not only hadn't he worked out anything "beforehand," but one wonders if he worked out anything at all about his relationship with his mother. What he experienced with his female supervisor, suddenly emerging from the hidden depths of his denial, was an image of his mother so powerfully critical, so disgusted with him—all superimposed on the face of a quite amiable supervisor. And he reacted as he never dared react while his mother was alive. He had brimmed over and there was no stopping the flow.

And this is—without particularly the drama in this situation—one of the consequences of refusing to deal not only with the inner image, the inner relationship, but denying the mother's death in order to keep the old relationship going just as it had gone in life.

The lost boy returns home. The angry boy lets loose.

The other way around—when there is as little denial as possible—brings with it a kind of warmth, a kind of soft sadness, and an acknowledged anger: I am angry that she's left me; I can be angry at her even though she died. A man can often regret that his mother is no longer present to share the good things in his life—but the relationship will still go on, in all its complexity.

It has to be mentioned here that most of the mental-health community treats the death of a mother in almost remarkably concrete terms. When a mother dies, the son is supposed to grieve, then must let her go somehow, as if her death truly ended something. I don't mean this in any seriously pejorative sense, because there are many schools of therapeutic thought that give credence to the mother as an "introjected object"—that is, it is admitted that mother lives within. But again, the focus will often be placed on the pathological aspects that result when mourning does not take place: the son identifies with the "lost object," becomes depressed, internalizes his anger, and thus deepens the depression. It is hard to tell whether the emphasis is on grieving for the actual loss of the person or for the loss of something deep inside.

I think the images may well blend: the outer death, the death of the concrete person, may well trigger thoughts and feelings of what one feels he has or hasn't received during life—and now there is no possibility of making up for it all, no possibility of gaining the love and gratification and acceptance that one has been searching for inside for so many years. I believe that the hope goes on—as I've tried to illus-

trate over and over in these pages—that a son keeps searching for that connection with his mother throughout his
life, working it without much consciousness into the fabric
of all his relationships with women, wives, lovers, friends.
And suddenly the death becomes symbolic of his inability
ever again to win these positive things. The death itself,
such a concrete final event, may become the symbol for a
kind of hopelessness that may even take the form of a
feeling that *no one* will ever love him the way she did.

Something within certainly does get *primed* to be altered—except in men whose dependency upon the living
woman has been quite infantile. I think it is a kind of panic
—the loss of the mother's world which she has formed inside a man, and now she is gone; she can no longer be tied
to the internal world, she can no longer give it support.
Perhaps the sense is that with her disappearance she has
taken the meaning of life away with her, has taken with
her the ingredients of the inner world, and a man is left
with a sense—momentary at best, total at worst—of a great
vast emptiness inside. I am reminded at this point of a state
called phantom-limb pain or sensation, in which a person
with, say, an amputated leg frequently feels that the leg is
still there: he can feel sensation in it, pain in it; in essence
he denies that it is gone.

A man severed from his mother by her death can experience himself as an amputee—the loss of a soul, the loss
of meaning, rather than the loss of a limb. Without my leg
I cannot walk without a crutch; without my mother perhaps I cannot live the same life I have been living without
the crutch of a substitute.

The loss that threatens a man when his mother dies
(and I think this is true no matter what feelings a man has

had for her—positive, negative, an ambivalent mixture of both) is the potential loss within, the threatened loss of a world, perhaps the loss of his very sense of existence. He must suddenly stand alone.

And so many feelings can result from this loss: guilt that he has somehow contributed to her death because he was not "good enough" to her (and sometimes in sleepless nights he recites a self-lacerating litany of the vicious and uncaring things he has done to her); a rage that she has created him and, like a departing god, has suddenly left; and all of it frequently being bound up in the depression resulting from the loss itself.

And here, as part of the growing out of it all, a man must realize that after all his way of life, his journey through the world of everyday reality, his every behavior, may all have been cut from a pattern, a template, and that he has been performing a life of obedience. Because the sense frequently is that *without her I am nothing*; she has gone and she promised me that she never would go, that I would have her always, that even the rages and bad feeling, not just the love and affection, were part and parcel of the bond, the attachment. And now she is gone. *And now I am nothing.* And who shall take her place, who shall be the person who will now fill me again with meaning? I must now be my own man or perish. The world is gone. Who will breathe life again into my soul so that I know I am alive?

It is all so unfair that a man can shake his fist toward the sky and curse God.

Rarely will men express these feelings to anyone but their therapists, and even then the expression is slow and halting: they will say that they feel silly, childish, for having such feelings as grown men. They feel shame. But the true power of it all is easily seen when a *son* dies: I have never met a woman who has ever become reconciled to the death of her son, even if she has been socially approved as a World War II gold-star mother.

It was over fifteen years ago and he went off and he died in the jungle somewhere, and they sent me a medal and a piece of paper that I've never read all through. And I've never gotten over it, and I never will get over it, and I curse the day I ever let him go.

I remember him when he was a baby and I remember him on the day when he appeared with those little gold bars on his shoulders, and the middle years seem vanished, as if he had never been. And what is there to make peace with? What reasons can ever give me the comfort that he died *for* something? And even if he really *did* die for something, what does it have to do with me, with him?

He's dead and I will never see him again. And part of me died with him.

And a son can say the same. Because from a reciprocal bond of such power, in the context of such loss, one can legitimately speak for the other. And the only way out of the darkness is to find some inner flame to rekindle, to take what she has given, breathe it in, and become reborn through the fire of an individual consciousness.

The divorce through death is never final. A man writes:

If only you could have known. If only you could have seen. There was a bond between us that God himself could never have loosened, and of course we both knew that but only you could say it, and of course I had to try to deny it because bonds that God himself

cannot loosen are fearful bonds, terrifying bonds, and
I had to try to break them or perish. But of course
I never broke them, I just said I had to, and I had to
keep trying to break them as if I really could. Pre-
tending you can is the thing that gives you heart,
makes you feel somehow that you are yourself. But I
never broke them, I never even came close. Even
when I saw the bond much more clearly than ever
before, all I could do was see it but I couldn't break it.
There was no choice. I could only accept what I saw.

What I would say to you now is that I would
never in my life have wanted you to be different—
not really, not at root. I would have wanted you to be
more accepting, to approve of everything I've done—
to sit back and nod and smile and to sacrifice everything you had to believe in to keep you going, sacrifice it to me so that I would never be alone, so that
I would never need anyone else in the world.

But you wouldn't give me that. And so I could
grow my own way. What you gave me instead was an
imagination, a firm conviction that I could understand many things but accept none of them, that life
was a weird twisting path without any hope ever of
security. I thank you for all of it, for the ability to
create my own reality, because no other reality could
ever do. And in that sense you let me create myself.

Wherever you are, understand that now. The war
is over.

He takes what he has written, folds it neatly in quarters,
and waits until family and friends have filed out of the
limousines headed for the cemetery. He goes to her coffin
and places the note under the rigid hands lying folded on

her breast, touches their iciness, then steps back and watches the men slowly close the lid. They look at him and he nods and they begin to wheel her away, and a line from a childhood prayer touches his memory.

"World without end," he says.

"Amen."

REFERENCES

CHAPTER ONE
Oedipal complex as a two-party interaction: John Weir Perry, *Roots of Renewal in Myth and Madness*. San Francisco: Jossey-Bass, 1976.

CHAPTER TWO
Marasmus: René A. Spitz, *The First Year of Life*. New York: International Universities Press, 1965.

Mother substitutes: H. F. Harlow and R. R. Zimmermann, "Affectional Responses in the Infant Monkey," *Science*, Vol. 130, p. 421.

The unconscious as mother: C. G. Jung, *Symbols of Transformation*. Volume 5 of *The Collected Works of C. G. Jung*. Princeton, N.J.: Princeton University Press, 1967, 1974.

CHAPTER THREE

Self-mutilation: Joseph Campbell, *The Masks of God: Primitive Mythology*. New York. Viking (Compass), 1970.

Murder of wife as mother substitute: John Balt, *By Reason of Insanity*. New York: New American Library, 1966.

CHAPTER FOUR

"Good-enough mothering": D. W. Winnicott, *The Maturational Processes and the Facilitating Environment*. New York: International Universities Press, 1965.

CHAPTER FIVE

Daily living out of myth: Joseph Campbell, *The Hero with a Thousand Faces*. Princeton, N.J.: Princeton University Press, 1968.

European feminists: "Down with Motherhood!" *Time*, July 28, 1980.

Matriarchal societies: Elizabeth Gould Davis, *The First Sex*. New York: Penguin, 1972.